starting SCIENCE

FOR SCOTLAND

BOOK TWO

OXFORD

UNIVERSITY PRESS

OXFORD
UNIVERSITY PRESS

Great Clarendon Street, Oxford OX2 6DP

Oxford University Press is a department of the University of Oxford.
It furthers the University's objective of excellence in research, scholarship,
and education by publishing worldwide in

Oxford New York

Auckland Bangkok Buenos Aires Cape Town Chennai
Dar es Salaam Delhi Hong Kong Istanbul Karachi Kolkata
Kuala Lumpur Madrid Melbourne Mexico City Mumbai Nairobi
São Paulo Shanghai Taipei Tokyo Toronto

Oxford is a registered trade mark of Oxford University Press
in the UK and in certain other countries

British Library Cataloguing in Publication Data

Data available

ISBN 0-19-914843-0

10 9 8 7 6 5 4 3 2 1

Typeset in Stone, Franklin Gothic, and Klepto
by IFA Design, Plymouth UK

Printed in Spain
by Gráficas Estella

Acknowledgements

The publisher would like to thank the following for their kind permission to
reproduce copyright material:

6 Scottish Viewpoint; **11l** Gustavo Tomsich/Corbis UK Ltd; **11c** Roger
Ressmeyer/Corbis UK Ltd; **11r** Roger Ressmeyer/Corbis UK Ltd; **11b** Johnson
Space Center/NASA; **12l** Roger Ressmeyer/Corbis UK Ltd; **12r** NASA;
12t Corbis UK Ltd; **12c** Corbis UK Ltd; **13t** National Air and Space Museum,
Smithsonian Institute (SI 99-15281-17); **13b** Johnson Space Center/NASA;
14t Corbis UK Ltd; **15t** NASA/Roger Ressmeyer/Corbis UK Ltd; **15b** John
Brenneis/Timepix/Rex Features; **16** . Tomkins/Scottish Viewpoint; **17cl** Galen
Rowell/Corbis UK Ltd; **17bl** Fraser/Oxford University ress; **17tr** Science Photo
Library; **17cr** Corbis UK Ltd; **18** Fraser/Oxford University Press; **19tl** Rex
Features; **19bl** Hulton-Deutsch Collection/Corbis UK Ltd; **19bc** Takeshi
Takahara/Science Photo Library; **19tr** George Hall/Corbis UK Ltd; **19br** Ford
Motor Company; **24l** NASA; **24r** NASA; **26t** Corbis UK Ltd; **26c** Phoebe
Dunn/Stock Connection, Inc./Alamy; **26b** NASA; **27** Chris Noble/Stone/Getty
Images; **28tl** Keren Su/Corbis UK Ltd; **28cl** Peter Brooker/Rex Features;
28cr Nils Joregensen/Rex Features; **28c** Lori Adamski Peek/Stone/Getty
Images; **28b** Zooid Pictures; **29** Adam Woolfitt/Corbis UK Ltd; **30tl** Corbis UK
Ltd; **30bl** Oxford University Press; **30tr** Sipa Press/Rex Features; **30br** Oxford
University Press; **31** Ricardo Arias/Latin Stock/Science Photo Library;
33tl CNRI/Science Photo Library; **33bl** Corbis UK Ltd; **33bc** Corbis UK Ltd;
33tr Science Photo Library; **33br** Corbis UK Ltd; **39** Oxford University Press;
41 Adam Woolfitt/Corbis UK Ltd; **42tl** Popperfoto/Alamy; **42tc** Leslie Garland /
LGPL/Alamy; **42tr** James L. Amos/Corbis UK Ltd; **42b** Lester V. Bergman/Corbis
UK Ltd; **43l** Martyn F. Chillmaid; **43r** Charles E. Rotkin/Corbis UK Ltd;
44t Andrew Lambert Photography/Science Photo Library; **44c** Zooid Pictures;
44b Oxford University Press; **45tl** Bettmann/Corbis UK Ltd; **45cl** Alfred

Pasieka/Science Photo Library; **45bl** Michael Barnett/Science Photo Library;
45tr Phil Schermeister/Corbis UK Ltd; **45cr** Maurice Nimmo; Frank Lane
Picture Agency/Corbis UK Ltd; **45br** Peter Gould; **46** Geoscience Features
Picture Library; **47cl** Scottish Viewpoint; **47bl** Sam Ogden/Science Photo
Library; **47tr** Chinch Gryniewicz; Ecoscene/Corbis UK Ltd;
47cr sciencephotos/Alamy; **48l** Roy Garner/Rex Features; **48r** Corbis UK Ltd;
49tl Flight Collection / Quadrant; **49cl** Larry Lee Photography/Corbis UK Ltd;
49bl Medical-on-Line; **49tr** Corbis UK Ltd; **49cr** Justin Kase/Alamy;
49br Genesis Space Photo Library; **49b** Werner Forman/Corbis UK Ltd;
52 Hulton/Archive/Getty Images; **53t** Lester V. Bergman/Corbis UK Ltd;
53b Andrew Lambert / LGPL/Alamy; **54** Camera Obscura and World of
Illusions; **55t** Oxford University Press; **55b** Philip Gould/Corbis UK Ltd;
56l Jose Luis Pelaez/Corbis UK Ltd; **56c** Scottish Viewpoint; **56r** Scottish
Viewpoint; **57bl** Morton Beebe/Corbis UK Ltd; **57br** Keren Su/Corbis UK Ltd;
57t Galen Rowell/Corbis UK Ltd; **57c** Martyn F. Chillmaid; **58tl** P. Gould/
Oxford University Press; **58bl** P. Gould/Oxford University Press; **58tr** Martyn
F. Chillmaid; **61t** Steve Bicknell/Alamy; **61b** Corbis UK Ltd; **62** Oxford
University Press; **65** Peter Gould; **68** Bettmann/Corbis UK Ltd; **69l** Dr Jeremy
Burgess/Science Photo Library; **69r** Martyn F. Chillmaid; **70l** Alan Towse;
Ecoscene/Corbis UK Ltd; **70r** Alan Towse; Ecoscene/Corbis UK Ltd; **71tl** Tim
Hill/Anthony Blake Photo Library; **71bl** Pete McArthur/Alamy; **71tr** Zooid
Pictures; **71br** Corbis UK Ltd; **72** Marlow Foods Ltd; **73l** Eye Of Science/
Science Photo Library; **73c** Eamonn Mcnulty/Science Photo Library;
73r Science Photo Library; **73b** Norm Thomas/Science Photo Library;
75l Ghislain & Marie David de Lossy /The Image Bank /Getty Images; **75r** Bob
Thomas/Alamy; **76t** Scottish Viewpoint; **76b** Holt Studios International;
77c Gary Braasch/Corbis UK Ltd; **77b** Corbis UK Ltd; **79** Ken Paterson/Scottish
Viewpoint; **81** Mehau Kulyk/Science Photo Library; **83l** Geophotos; **83r** Peter
Ryan/Science Photo Library; **85l** Archivo Iconografico, S.A./Corbis UK Ltd;
85c Imaging Body; **85r** NASA; **87l** Oxford University Press; **87c** Michael
Howes/The Garden Picture Library/Alamy; **87r** Oxford University Press;
89cl Martyn F. Chillmaid; **89l** Martyn F. Chillmaid; **89cr** Martyn F. Chillmaid;
89r Andrew Lambert Photography/Science Photo Library; **89t** Roger
Ressmeyer/Corbis UK Ltd; **89b** Martyn F. Chillmaid; **90l** Gillette Group UK Ltd;
90c Cc Studio/Science Photo Library; **90r** Siemens AG; **91tl** Zooid Pictures;
91cl Zooid Pictures; **91tr** Andrew Laenen/Rex Features; **91cr** Ian Harwood;
Ecoscene/Corbis UK Ltd; **91c** Zooid Pictures; **91b** Emitec, Inc;
92 Rune Hellestad/Corbis UK Ltd; **93** Edinburgh University Library; **95l** Alex
Bartel/Science Photo Library; **95r** Martin Bond/Science Photo Library;
96 Fraser/Oxford University Press; **97t** Novastock/ Stock Connection,
Inc./Alamy; **97c** Canon (UK) Ltd; **97b** Will & Deni Mcintyre/Science Photo
Library; **98** Sandy Felsenthal/Corbis UK Ltd; **99t** Oxford University Press;
99c Jerry Mason/Science Photo Library; **99b** Goodrich Fuel & Utility Systems;
100t Ed Young/Corbis UK Ltd; **100c** Geoff Tompkinson/Science Photo Library;
100b Lester Lefkowitz/Corbis UK Ltd; **102** Ford Motor Company (UK); **103l**
Siemens AG; **103c** Zooid Pictures; **103r** GRANADA TELEVISION; **104** Roger
Tidman/Corbis UK Ltd; **105** Andrew Brown; Ecoscene/Corbis UK Ltd;
106t Anthony Cooper; Ecoscene/Corbis UK Ltd; **106tr** Corbis UK Ltd; **106c**
JosephSohm; ChromoSohm Inc./Corbis UK Ltd; **106b** P.Tomkins/VisitScotland/
Scottish Viewpoint; **107tl** David T. Grewcock; Frank Lane Picture Agency/
Corbis UK Ltd; **107bl** Maximilian Stock Ltd/Science Photo Library;
107tc Corbis UK Ltd; **107bc** Corbis UK Ltd; **107tr** Bsip, M.i.g.0baeza/Science
Photo Library; **107br** Paul A. Souders/Corbis UK Ltd; **108tl** Steve Austin;
Papilio/Corbis UK Ltd; **108tr** Corbis UK Ltd; **108b** David Kjaer/Worldwide
Picture Library/Alamy; **109tl** Corbis UK Ltd; **109tc** Anthony Bannister; Gallo
Images/Corbis UK Ltd; **109tr** Corbis UK Ltd; **109b** W. Perry Conway/Corbis UK
Ltd; **110t** David Cayless/Oxford Scientific Films; **110c** Corbis UK Ltd;
110b Lynda Richardson/Corbis UK Ltd; **111tl** Holt Studios International;
111bl Andrew Brown; Ecoscene/Corbis UK Ltd; **111tc** Frank Blackburn;
Ecoscene/Corbis UK Ltd; **111bc** Sally A. Morgan; Ecoscene/Corbis UK Ltd;
111tr Andrew Brown; Ecoscene/Corbis UK Ltd; **111br** Wild Country/Corbis
UK Ltd; **112** Sally A. Morgan; Ecoscene/Corbis UK Ltd; **113t** Corbis UK Ltd;
113b Tony Gervis/Robert Harding Picture Library Ltd/Alamy; **114t** Brian
Mitchell/Photofusion Picture Library/Alamy; **114c** Mauro Fermariello/Science
Photo Library; **114b** Jamie Harron; Papilio/Corbis UK Ltd; **115** Dougie
Pincock; **116l** Roger Ressmeyer/Corbis UK Ltd; **116r** NASA; **117** Scottish
Viewpoint; **119** Zooid Pictures; **120l** Rex Features; **120r** Susumu
Nishinaga/Science Photo Library; **120c** Charles O'Rear/Corbis UK Ltd;
120b Gusto/Science Photo Library; **123** Zooid Pictures; **124tl** Mark
Bacon/Alamy; **124bl** Science Photo Library; **124tc** Ralph A. Clevenger/Corbis
UK Ltd; **124bc** Pictor International/ ImageState/Alamy; **124tr** Jonathan
Blair/Corbis UK Ltd; **124br** Nigel Cattlin/ Holt Studios International Ltd/Alamy

Introduction

Introducing this book...

Your science class is a place for doing experiments. From your previous science lessons you will already know some of the things scientists do. Every day scientists carry out experiments, trying to find the answers to many different problems. In fact, science is really all about doing experiments.

But your science class is also a place for reading books. Scientists spend lots of time reading books, searching for information, looking up instructions about how to do experiments, finding out what other scientists have done. You need to practise this skill too.

Starting Science for Scotland students' book has been written to be your course 'companion' while you are studying science in S1 and S2. It has a number of jobs to do. And it has been written especially to help you:

- ➲ to understand what you find out in your own experiments
- ➲ to develop further your scientific thinking skills
- ➲ to see more where science fits into everyday life, how important science is, and how much scientists have been able to improve the world we all live in

...and how to use it

Starting Science for Scotland is made up of units. Most units contain three pages:

- ➲ **Starting off** is the first page. In it, you will learn a new piece of science. You should begin with this page. Otherwise, the other pages may not make any sense.
- ➲ **Going further** is the second page. It follows on from what you learned in Starting off.
- ➲ **For the enthusiast**, the third page, takes you even further. The material on it is usually more difficult.

When you start to work on a page, you should first read everything **thoroughly – including Did you know**. You should also look carefully at any diagrams. Then you can answer the questions. Some questions end with a triangle sign (▲). This tells you that the answer to the question is written somewhere on the page. Some questions begin **Try to find out**. You will usually have to look through other books – like encyclopaedias – for the answers to these. To answer the other questions, you will have to use what you have learned on the page and a bit of brain power! Using your brain is all part of *Starting Science for Scotland*. In Chapter 20 you will find something different – it's all about real-world science contexts past, present, and future.

In writing *Starting Science for Scotland*, we have also tried to find things which will interest you, and things which you will enjoy doing. We hope that we have succeeded!

Alan Fraser
David Coppock
Anthony Partridge

Contents

Scotland's first Astronomer Royal, Thomas Henderson, was born on 28th December 1798, in Dundee, and educated at Dundee Academy. In Edinburgh he had access to the Observatory of the Astronomical Institution on Calton Hill. But he had poor eyesight, and decided to concentrate on mathematical astronomy rather than observing.

In 1830 he compiled a list of stars for Sir John Ross's Arctic expedition. (Ross was another Scot who searched for the great North-West Passage, and who captained the expedition on which his nephew discovered the North Magnetic Pole in May/June 1831.)

Henderson was appointed the first Astronomer Royal in Scotland in 1834, and worked at the Observatory for ten years, making more than 60 000 observations of star positions. Whilst working there he became the first person to calculate the position of a star in the sky (*Alpha Centauri* at 3.25 light years – this has now been recalculated at around 4.5 light years). Because Henderson delayed the publication of his results Friedrich Wilhelm Bessel is credited with publishing the first position of a star (*61 Cygni*).

He died on 23 November 1844 and is buried in Greyfriars Churchyard, Edinburgh. There is a memorial tablet to him on the west side of the Playfair Building (Royal Scottish Academy).

This is our **Solar System**. It is made up of the Sun and the planets, comets, and asteroids that travel round it. Earth is one of the planets. The Sun is at the centre of the Solar System. It provides all the planets with light and heat, and it holds the Solar System together. The planets are moving very fast, but they don't fly off into space. The force of gravity between the Sun and the planets keeps the planets in their orbits. These orbits are elliptical.

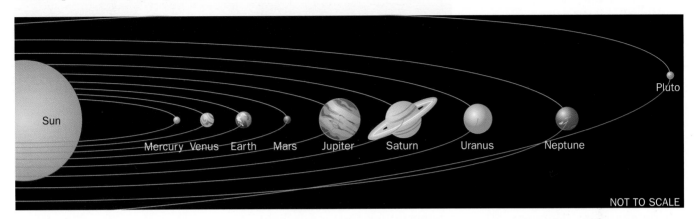

Sun · Mercury · Venus · Earth · Mars · Jupiter · Saturn · Uranus · Neptune · Pluto

NOT TO SCALE

Years...

The length of time taken for a planet to go round the Sun once (i.e. to complete a full orbit) is called a year. Different planets have different sizes of orbits and so they have different lengths of year. Earth is 150 million kilometres from the Sun and takes (approximately) 365 days to go round the Sun once. The length of Earth's year is 365 days. Pluto, the furthest planet, has a far bigger orbit. It is 10 billion km away from the Sun and takes 90 500 Earth days to go round the Sun once. Its year is therefore 90 500 days long.

...and days

As well as travelling round the Sun, the Earth spins (like a spinning top). We call the time our part of the Earth gets light from the Sun *'day'* and the time when we get no light *'night'*. In science, however, one day is the length of time it takes for a planet to spin once. For Earth, it is very nearly 24 hours (23.93 h to be exact). We say that one day has 24 hours.

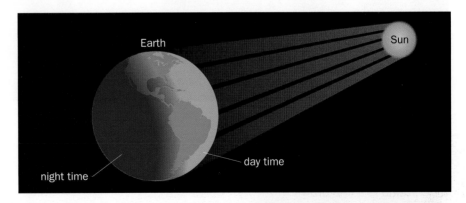

Earth · Sun · day time · night time

1 What is the Solar System made up of? ▲

2 What is an orbit? Which of the planets has the biggest orbit? ▲

3 How are the planets kept in orbit round the Sun? ▲

4 What is meant by a year? Which planet has the longest year? ▲

5 Explain what is meant by saying that Earth's day is 24 hours long. ▲

6 **Try to find out:**
a why leap years are needed
b what is special about Pluto's orbit
c the name of a comet.

DiD YOU KNOW?

➲ Asteroids are lumps of space rock. The biggest measures 940 km across.

➲ Comets are huge masses of ice and rock in the outer Solar System. We only see them when they come close to the Sun.

When you are thinking about the spinning Earth, it's useful to imagine two things:

1 **that the Earth is spinning round a line drawn through the North and South poles.** (We call this the axis)
2 **when this axis is compared with the Earth's orbit, it is at a tilt.** In other words, the Earth is tilted with respect to the Sun.

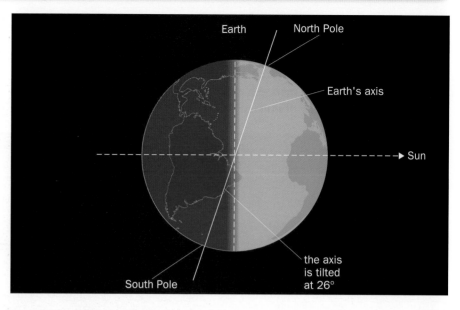

Earth   North Pole

Earth's axis

Sun

South Pole

the axis is tilted at 26°

If you look at the diagram below, you can see how this explains the changing seasons. (Summers with warm temperatures and long daylight, winters colder with less daylight.)

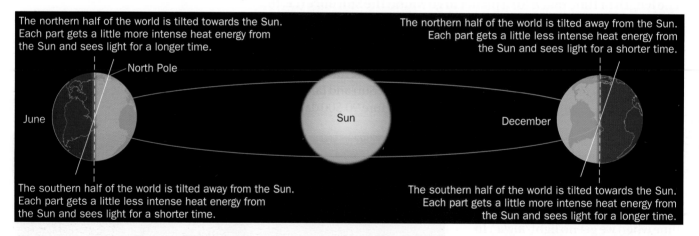

The northern half of the world is tilted towards the Sun. Each part gets a little more intense heat energy from the Sun and sees light for a longer time.

North Pole

June

Sun

The southern half of the world is tilted away from the Sun. Each part gets a little less intense heat energy from the Sun and sees light for a shorter time.

The northern half of the world is tilted away from the Sun. Each part gets a little less intense heat energy from the Sun and sees light for a shorter time.

December

The southern half of the world is tilted towards the Sun. Each part gets a little more intense heat energy from the Sun and sees light for a longer time.

1 Copy out and complete
  a The axis which Earth spins round is a line drawn
    _____ ▲
  b As it goes round the Sun, Earth is tilted _____ ▲
2 Which part of the Earth is tilted towards the Sun in
  a June
  b December?
  How does this affect the temperature and the daylight? ▲

3 Why is Christmas likely to be warmer in Australia than in Britain?
4 Imagine that you lived in an Arctic village. Then write a paragraph about what life would be like
  a in summer
  b in winter.
5 **Try to find out:**
  a how the *Land of the Midnight Sun* got its name
  b what the Northern Lights are.

DID YOU KNOW?

⮑ The effects are greatest at the Poles. In the Arctic Circle, there is no darkness in the summer. In winter, some north Canadian villages don't see the sun rise for 4 months.

When the light goes out

The phases of the Moon

The Moon is a giant sphere which orbits the Earth. It does not make light on its own. You see it because it reflects the light of the Sun. But you don't always see the same shape of Moon. This is because:

1 You can only see the side of the Moon which is lit by the Sun
2 As the Moon orbits the Earth, the amount of the lit side of the Moon which *you can see* changes

The Moon takes roughly 30 days to orbit the Earth. Every week, we see the Moon in a different place in the sky. As the diagram shows, that's why it seems to have different shapes.

Eclipses

An eclipse takes place when one planet or moon blocks off light from another.

A **solar eclipse** takes place when the Moon gets directly between the Sun and the Earth. The Moon blocks out the Sun's light from part of the Earth. As long as the eclipse lasts, this produces a shadow on that part of the Earth.

In a **lunar eclipse**, the same type of thing happens, except this time the Earth blocks off the light from reaching the Moon by being directly between it and the Sun.

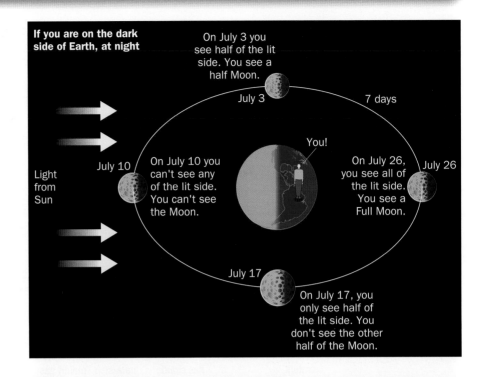

If you are on the dark side of Earth, at night

On July 3 you see half of the lit side. You see a half Moon.

July 3 7 days

Light from Sun

July 10

On July 10 you can't see any of the lit side. You can't see the Moon.

You!

On July 26, you see all of the lit side. You see a Full Moon.

July 26

July 17

On July 17, you only see half of the lit side. You don't see the other half of the Moon.

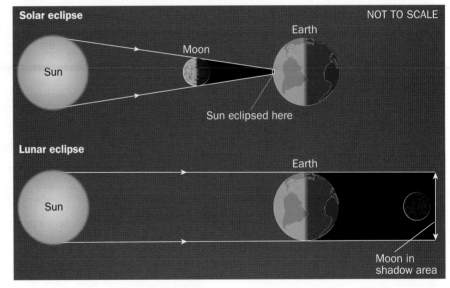

Solar eclipse NOT TO SCALE

Earth
Moon
Sun
Sun eclipsed here

Lunar eclipse

Earth
Sun
Moon in shadow area

QUESTIONS

1 Why do you see the Moon? Why do you not always see the same shape of Moon? ▲
2 a How long does the Moon take to orbit the Earth? ▲
  b Where is the Moon in its orbit when there is a full Moon? ▲
3 What happens when there is a solar eclipse? How is it different from a lunar eclipse?
4 In an eclipse, the shadow strikes the Earth for a long time, but people can only see it for a few minutes. Why is this?
5 **Try to find out:**
  a where the next solar eclipse will be, and when
  b how animals and birds are affected by an eclipse.

DID YOU KNOW?

➲ The earliest reported eclipse was in China in 2134 B.C. It was thought that a giant dragon had eaten the Sun. Archers shot arrows into the air and many drummers beat their drums to scare away the dragon.

	Mercury	Venus	Earth	Mars	Jupiter	Saturn	Uranus	Neptune	Pluto
Average distance to Sun	60 million km	108 million km	150 million km	230 million km	780 million km	1400 million km	2900 million km	4500 million km	5900 million km
Time for one orbit (in Earth time)	88 days	225 days	365.25 days	687 days	12 years	29 years	84 years	165 years	248 years
Time for the planet to rotate once	59 days	243 days	23 hrs 56 mins	24 hrs 30 mins	10 hrs	10 hrs 15 mins	11 hrs	16 hrs	6.5 days
Diameter (kilometres)	5 000 km	12 000 km	12 750 km	7 000 km	140 000 km	120 000 km	52 000 km	50 000 km	3 000 km
What is the surface like?	rocky with lots of craters	rocky has clouds	rocky with water has clouds	rocky with lots of craters	outer layers are mainly gas	outer layers are mainly gas	outer layers are mainly gas	outer layers are mainly gas	rocky
Average temperature	350 °C day -170 °C night	480 °C	22 °C	-23 °C	-150 °C at cloud top	-180 °C at cloud top	-210 °C at cloud top	-220 °C at cloud top	-230 °C
What are the main gases in the atmosphere?	almost none traces of helium, argon	carbon dioxide	nitrogen oxygen	carbon dioxide argon nitrogen	hydrogen helium methane ammonia	hydrogen helium methane ammonia	hydrogen helium methane	hydrogen helium methane	?
How many satellites (moons) does it have?	0	0	1	2	20+ (rings also)	20+ (rings also)	22+ (rings also)	8	1
First space mission	1974 flyby	1962 flyby 1978 probe		1964 flyby 1971 probe	1972 flyby 1995 probe	1973 flyby 2004? probe	1977 flyby	1977 flyby	2017 flyby

flyby = spacecraft flew past, collecting data   **probe** = spacecraft sent a probe to the planet surface to collect data

QUESTIONS

1 What is
  a the distance from the Sun to Pluto
  b the biggest planet's diameter
  c the temperature on Venus
  d the length of a day on Mars? ▲
2 Which planet has
  a the longest 'day'
  b the shortest year
  c the highest temperature
  d the biggest number of moons? ▲
3 Which planet was the first to have information sent back to Earth from
  a a spacecraft which flew past
  b a spacecraft which landed? ▲
4 Suggest, giving your reasons
  a which planet is most like Earth
  b why Mercury, Venus, Earth and Mars are considered as one group of planets and Jupiter, Saturn, Uranus and Neptune as another group.
5 **Try to find out** all you can about Mars and Venus.

DID YOU KNOW?
➲ The pressure of Jupiter's atmosphere is so great that any probe is crushed 200 km above its surface.
➲ Venus rotates 'backwards'; there, the Sun rises in the west.

It's amazing to think that we have information about planets billions of kilometres away from Earth! How did **astronomers** (scientists who study stars and planets) find out about our Solar System?

Earliest astronomers collected much of their information using simple telescopes. Much improved telescopes are still highly useful today.

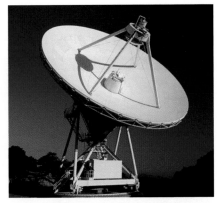

Simple optical telescopes using lenses allowed:
- ➲ Galileo to discover Jupiter's moons and spots on the surface of the Sun (1609)
- ➲ a new planet (Uranus) to be discovered (1781)
- ➲ the distance to a star to be measured (1838). Lots of complicated maths was involved!

Earth-based telescopes have a big disadvantage. Their work is affected by dust and other substances in the atmosphere. This blocks some signals from space and blurs others. Light from the Sun also affects the work of optical (astronomical) telescopes.

Today's optical telescopes are much bigger and more complicated. Using large mirrors instead of lenses, they focus the light onto detectors. In this way they can detect very weak beams of light from distant stars. Computers use the signals to make better images.

Many objects in space e.g. hot stars send out radio waves. These can be detected by radio telescopes. These telescopes also focus the rays onto detectors, but they are more powerful. For one thing, they can be built much larger. For another, signals from a number of radio telescopes can be added together to strengthen the signal.

The *Hubble* space telescope overcomes these problems. The telescope orbits Earth every 96 minutes and is controlled from the ground. Its cameras are like digital cameras. They detect light using electronic detectors and the signals are beamed to Earth. *Hubble* has provided huge amounts of data and allows astronomers to explore the furthest parts of the Universe.

QUESTIONS

1 What is detected by
   a an optical telescope
   b a radiotelescope? ▲
2 How are modern optical telescopes better than older ones? ▲
3 What is the major problem with optical telescopes used from the Earth? How does *Hubble* overcome this problem? ▲
4 Find three ways in which electronics and computers help astronomers.
5 Why is it safe to use an optical telescope to look at the Moon but **extremely dangerous** to use one to look at the Sun (and you must not do it)?
6 **Try to find out:**
   a more about Galileo's work
   b where the biggest Earth-controlled telescopes are, and why.

DiD YOU KNOW?
- ➲ The most powerful optical telescope could detect the light from a candle 24 000 km away.
- ➲ *Hubble*'s focusing system is so accurate, it could focus on a 10p coin 300 km away.

Information from telescopes is invaluable. *Hubble*'s information helps astronomers decide on a star's temperature, age, and what it is made up of. But the best way to get information about the planets in our Solar System is to send a space probe to find out. Most of these space probes are unmanned rockets full of scientific instruments. Some have flown past planets. A few have landed on them. Humans have not yet visited any planet but American astronauts landed on the Moon in 1969.

Here are a few of these space probes and some of the data they collected.

DID YOU KNOW?
⮕ The Jupiter probe only lasted 59 minutes before it was crushed and vapourised by Jupiter's atmosphere.

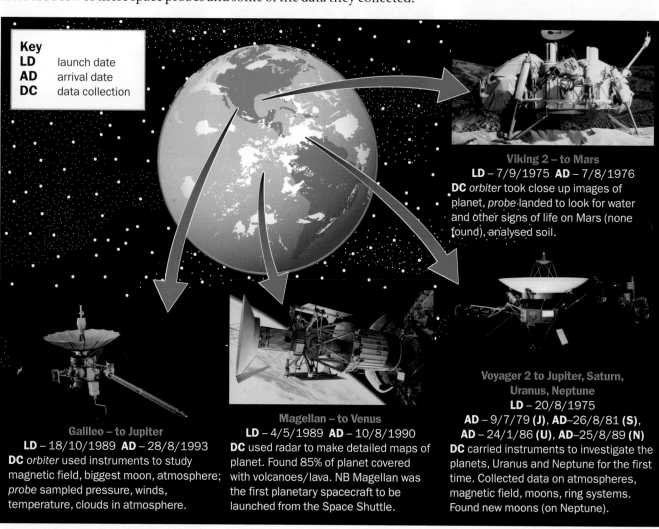

Key
LD launch date
AD arrival date
DC data collection

Viking 2 – to Mars
LD – 7/9/1975 **AD** – 7/8/1976
DC *orbiter* took close up images of planet, *probe* landed to look for water and other signs of life on Mars (none found), analysed soil.

Galileo – to Jupiter
LD – 18/10/1989 **AD** – 28/8/1993
DC *orbiter* used instruments to study magnetic field, biggest moon, atmosphere; *probe* sampled pressure, winds, temperature, clouds in atmosphere.

Magellan – to Venus
LD – 4/5/1989 **AD** – 10/8/1990
DC used radar to make detailed maps of planet. Found 85% of planet covered with volcanoes/lava. NB Magellan was the first planetary spacecraft to be launched from the Space Shuttle.

Voyager 2 to Jupiter, Saturn, Uranus, Neptune
LD – 20/8/1975
AD – 9/7/79 **(J)**, **AD**–26/8/81 **(S)**, **AD** – 24/1/86 **(U)**, **AD**–25/8/89 **(N)**
DC carried instruments to investigate the planets, Uranus and Neptune for the first time. Collected data on atmospheres, magnetic field, moons, ring systems. Found new moons (on Neptune).

1 Where did Viking 2 fly? How long was its flight? What information did it send back? ▲
2 Which of the space craft landed on a planet and which flew past? ▲
3 What did Magellan discover? What was special about its launch? ▲
4 Draw a diagram (to scale) to show the distances which Voyager 2 travelled from Earth to each of the planets on its journey. Then add to your diagram the time it took to travel from one planet to the next.
5 **Try to find out** which space flights are taking place at the minute. (Use NASA – the North American Space Agency – to help you.)

Manned spaceflight

It's a long time since the first manned spaceflight. In 1961, a Russian cosmonaut, Yuri Gagarin, orbited Earth. Soon afterwards, US and Russian astronauts were orbiting Earth regularly. The first spacewalk took place in 1968. Then attention turned to the Moon. American astronauts flew to the Moon and orbited it in 1968. The spacescraft, Apollo 11, finally landed there on July 20, 1969. A few missions to the Moon followed that, but they ended in 1972. Since then, space scientists have concentrated on working in space around Earth. Scientific space stations have been built to orbit the Earth. Spacecraft, like the Space Shuttle, fly people and equipment to and from the stations. These space stations have allowed a huge amount of information to be collected about the Earth, about its surface and its climate, and about space. The stations have also allowed scientists to carry out useful experiments under **zero gravity** conditions.

The three astronauts from Apollo 11: Michael Collins, Neil Armstrong (the first man to set foot on the Moon), Buzz Aldrin

Zero gravity

If you have ever been in a roller coaster, you may know what it feels like to be under zero or near-zero gravity. At the top of the ride, gravity makes you press down on your seat. When the roller coaster drops, gravity still pulls you down but you don't press on the seat so hard because the seat is dropping also. The roller coaster and you are falling at the same speed. You feel as if you have *no weight*.

An orbiting space station is affected by gravity. It makes the station (and everything in it) fall *towards* Earth. As it is travelling so fast, however, the station does not fall *to* Earth but stays in its orbit. Because the station and its contents are falling towards Earth at the same speed, everything in the station behaves as if it has no weight and is under zero gravity.

Scientists are very keen to do experiments in zero gravity conditions. Under zero gravity, crystals grow perfectly, plants and our bodies grow differently, and some chemicals react differently. Experiments in space will grow pure crystals for superfast computers and help to develop new materials, medicines, and foods.

Zero gravity at work

QUESTIONS

1 Why are
   a Yuri Gargarin
   b Neil Armstrong famous? ▲
2 What jobs are done by
   a the Space Shuttle
   b space stations? ▲
3 Why does gravity not make a space station fall to Earth? ▲
4 Are astronauts affected by gravity in a space station? Why do they seem to be weightless? ▲
5 Why is 'zero gravity' important to scientists? ▲
6 **Try to find out:**
   a how some of the difficulties in space travel are overcome
   b what happened on Apollo 13.

DiD YOU KNOW?

Some difficulties in space travel, all caused by zero gravity

⊃ eating (food floats, so do left-over crumbs!

⊃ floating away when sleeping

⊃ washing (no baths, no showers)

⊃ cleaning teeth (no spitting allowed!)

⊃ going to the toilet

⊃ mid-air rubbish

The Universe is massive, so big that astronomers have had to invent a new unit to measure distances in it. That unit is the **light year, the distance that light travels in 1 year (9.46 million million kilometres).** As you read this page, you will realise why a new unit was needed.

Our Solar System is very big – it is 15 billion km across. The Sun at the centre is a giant mass of gases. The gases are constantly reacting in nuclear reactions which provide huge amounts of heat and light. That makes the Sun like many other stars and, in fact, the Sun is a star. There are countless numbers of stars – even in our **galaxy**.

Saturn storm: taken by *Hubble* space camera

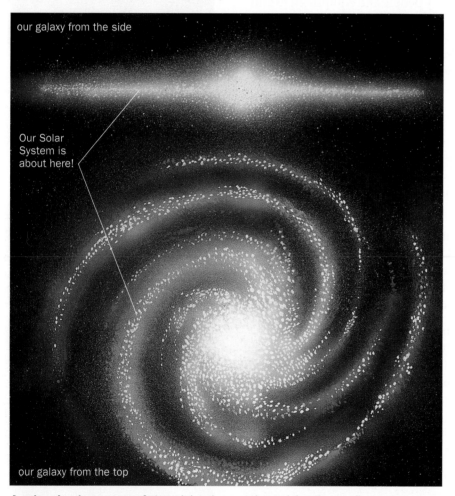

our galaxy from the side

Our Solar System is about here!

our galaxy from the top

A galaxy is a huge mass of stars. It has been estimated that the smallest galaxy contains 100 000 stars and the largest, 3000 billion.
Our galaxy is called the Milky Way galaxy. It is thought to have a sphere at its centre, with 4 spiral arms coming from it, and to be 100 000 light years across. You can't see the centre of the galaxy because of space dust clouds. Scientists have used radio waves and infra-red (heat) waves to try to work out a picture of it.

The **Universe** is even bigger still! We use the word 'Universe' to mean everything that exists. Astronomers have estimated that it contains 100 billion galaxies each with 100 billion stars. But these are guesses! All you can say for sure is that it is massive and that it stretches further than anyone can possibly imagine and, of course, that you live on a planet that is a tiny, tiny, but very important part of it.

DiD YOU KNOW?
- Constellations are groups of bright stars that seem to form patterns when they are viewed from Earth. There are 88 in all.

1 What is a light year? How big is it? ▲
2 How big do astronomers estimate our Solar System to be? ▲
3 What is our Sun like? How does it keep giving out heat energy? ▲
4 What is a galaxy? Write down some details about our galaxy.
5 What do we mean by the Universe? How many stars do scientists think that there are in the Universe (roughly!)?
6 **Try to find out** what is meant by
   a red giant
   b white dwarf stars.

Space is not just made up of planets and stars like our Sun with empty space in between. The information that scientists have collected has suggested that space contains far more than that. Some of the information allows astronomers to say for sure that things exist. They can, for example, see stars many light years away. But sometimes they only have enough information to suggest a theory. After that, the next task is to find more information to back up, or change, the theory.

Black holes

Astronomers think that black holes are objects left over from collapsing stars. Like our Sun, stars are giant masses of reacting hydrogen. The star's gravity pulls the gases inwards. The immense heat produced when the hydrogen in the star's core reacts creates a great pressure outwards. When the star runs out of hydrogen to burn (as all stars do), there is no outward pressure. Gravity pulls all the matter in the star inwards, creating a very very dense object with extremely strong gravity. This is a **black hole**.

The gravity is so strong that a black hole pulls in everything that is near it. Not even light can escape, and so no one can see a black hole. The *Hubble* telescope, however, can measure the speed of gases swirling around a black hole, and X-rays that can escape from one, and the information from this has helped build up the model we have today.

False colour photo of dust swirling around a black hole

An expanding Universe and the Big Bang theory

In 1929, Edwin Hubble discovered that light from distant galaxies was *redder* than would have been predicted. Since light from objects that are moving away had been found to be redder than expected, he suggested that the galaxies must be moving outwards. Hubble suggested that the Universe must be expanding. The question was 'From what?'

Hubble's findings gave support to the **Big Bang** theory of the formation of the Universe which was being considered at the time. Put very simply, the theory suggests that, billions of years ago, the Universe we now know was only a few millimetres in size. Then everything exploded and moved outwards – and is still moving outwards. Scientists have since suggested that, first, a fireball of gases was formed. Then the gases cooled and condensed, eventually forming stars and planets.

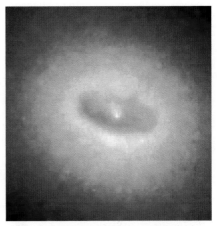

Edwin Hubble

There is evidence to support some of that theory, but there are questions it cannot answer. What was there before the **Big Bang**? How could everything be made from something so small? If the Universe was so small once, what was there for it to expand into? There are many mysteries left in space!

1 What is a black hole and why did it get its name? ▲
2 What evidence is there that black holes exist? What makes astronomers think that there is a black hole in our galaxy? ▲
3 Astronomers talk about 'an expanding Universe'. What evidence is there for this? ▲
4 What does the Big Bang theory suggest? What questions can this theory not answer?

DID YOU KNOW?

➲ Astronomers saw clouds of dust and stars swirling very fast round the centre of the Milky Way. That made them think that there is a black hole at the centre of our galaxy. They launched a space telescope – Chandra – to investigate and found that there is!

Forces

Forces are pushes, pulls, and twists. Forces can speed things up. They can slow things down. Forces can change the direction of things. Sometimes, forces can do two or three of these things at the same time. If no forces are acting on an object then one of two things will happen. If it is stationary, it will remain stationary. If it is moving, it will continue to move at the same speed in a straight line. Forces can make things happen. The bigger the force, the bigger the effect. In this chapter you will learn more about the effects of these forces, and how you can measure them.

There is no such thing as a completely smooth surface. There are some highly polished surfaces which seem to be perfectly smooth. But if you look at these surfaces with a microscope, you can see that even they have rough edges. The rubbing of these rough edges causes the force called **friction**.

Friction is the force produced when two surfaces rub on each other. Friction tries to stop the surfaces from sliding over one another. The force of friction is small for fairly smooth surfaces like glass and ice. It is much greater for rough surfaces like sandpaper or concrete.

Friction can be useful. You couldn't walk without friction. Friction prevents the soles of your shoes from slipping over the ground. And with no friction your bicycle brakes wouldn't stop you.

When you write with a pencil, friction rubs millions of carbon atoms off the end of the pencil. That's what leaves the black mark on the paper.

When you rub wood with sandpaper, the high friction removes imperfections in the wood.

Friction can cause problems. Then it has to be made smaller. When the moving parts of machines rub on each other, they are worn away by friction. The machine is slowed down too. That's why machines have to be **lubricated** with oil or grease. Lubricating cuts down friction. A well oiled machine runs more smoothly, and lasts longer. Oiling the hinges on a door cuts down friction and makes the door swing more easily.

Feel how smooth the page is – this is what it looks like under a microscope.

Rubber-soled boots produce more friction to give climbers a better grip.

The surface of the slide has to be as smooth as possible to reduce friction.

Cutting down friction – to make the wheels run smoothly.

DID YOU KNOW?

➲ Skiers wax their skis to cut down friction.

➲ Teflon, which is used to coat non-stick frying pans, is a low friction material.

1 Make lists of surfaces which are
   a high friction
   b low friction. ▲
2 Make two lists to show when friction needs to be
   a as high as possible
   b as low as possible. ▲
3 Compare the effect of sliding a small wooden block, a rubber eraser and an ice cube across a smooth floor. What can you say about the amount of friction and the distance travelled?
4 Why does a bicycle chain need to be
   a cleaned
   b lubricated? ▲
5 Why will a pencil write on paper but not on glass?
6 Compare the effect of running and stopping on a shiny gym floor in your socks and in rubber-soled trainers.
7 What causes a dry door hinge to squeak?
   How would you cure it?

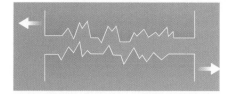

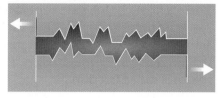

Friction is caused by the roughness of the two surfaces. When the high points catch on each other, this stops the surfaces from sliding smoothly against each other. Friction is high.

When the surfaces are smooth, there are no high points to catch against each other, and the surfaces slide easily. Friction is low.

Friction can be reduced by lubrication. The oil or grease forces the surfaces apart. This separates the high points of each surface so that they can slide across each other.

Tyres grip the road by friction. That's what allows the driver to speed up, turn and brake safely. Strangely, when the weather is dry, new and worn tyres work nearly as well as each other. But when it is raining, the water lubricates the 'footprint' of the tyre where it touches the road. This forces the tyre away from the road, and skidding can start. In a new tyre, the grooves in the tread pattern channel the water away from the footprint to reduce the lubricating effect and to prevent skidding.

Measuring roughness

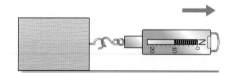

Students are comparing the roughness of two shoe soles, a trainer's rubber sole and a leather shoe sole. They increase the slope until slipping starts. At that point, the downwards force due to the weight of the shoe just matches the upwards force of the friction.

Students are measuring the force needed to pull a block along different floor coverings. The block has one smooth surface, one surface covered in fine sandpaper, one surface covered in rough sandpaper.

Tyres grip the road by friction. But some do this better than others.

QUESTIONS

1 Draw a trainer and shoe on a slope as above. Draw in arrows to show the forces acting along the slope
   a before slipping starts
   b after slipping starts.
   Predict which shoe will slip first. Why is this? ▲
2 In the experiment (right, above) the students pull the block along wood, vinyl, and carpet. If the force for pulling fine sandpaper along wood is 10 newtons, predict whether

the results for the other faces and surfaces will be higher or lower. How many measurements will they need to make? ▲
3 Why is it important for there to be a large amount of friction
   a between car tyres and the road
   b between brake pads and the wheel? ▲
4 **a** Why do car wheels spin on icy roads?
   b Why does gritting the road help to prevent this?
5 Why is braking more difficult on wet roads than on dry?

DID YOU KNOW?

➲ Tyres on racing cars work differently. In the dry, a 'slick' tyre with no tread pattern is used. But the tread is made from a special type of rubber which gets sticky when hot. This adds extra friction between the car and the road.

➲ A new car tyre travelling at 50 mph can displace 40 litres of water every second.

➲ A new car tyre has 8 mm tread depth. It is illegal to drive a car with a tyre tread less than 1.6 mm deep.

Friction doesn't only happen when solids rub together. When an object moves through a fluid (a liquid or a gas) friction also takes place.

The amount of resistance to something moving through a fluid depends on its shape. Imagine you're at the swimming baths. It is difficult to walk fast through the water, because the whole of the front of your body has to push the water aside. It's much easier to move when swimming. Then only your head and shoulders have to push through the water. The rest of your body follows along behind! You are more streamlined in this position.

In 'free-fall' (before the parachute has opened,) the parachutist can reach a high constant speed. The small area of a human body slips easily through the air. Once the chute opens, the speed reduces to a much slower steady speed. It is much more difficult for the large area of the parachute to slip through the air. It is as though the air rubbing against the parachute produces friction. Air resistance increases when the area is large.

Low air resistance, high speed of fall

The large parachute reduces the speed of fall.

Streamlining

Eighty years ago, car design was in its early stages. Speed (and therefore air resistance) was not important.

Wind tunnel tests are now used to improve the streamlining of cars. Smooth, round surfaces cut friction and reduce air resistance.

Modern cars are streamlined. This reduces fuel consumption. They therefore pollute the environment less.

1 Students make model parachutes to investigate how they work. They make large parachutes and small ones. They attach them to heavy loads and light loads. What things do you think will affect the rate of fall? Try to explain why these are so. What other variables might they consider?

2 Look at photographs of cars and planes over the last 100 years. Does the change in shape have anything in common for cars and planes? Why is this?

3 In the drawing opposite, students are investigating the effect that the shape of an object has on how quickly it falls through a liquid. Describe how they might do the experiment. What kind of shapes do you think will fall the quickest? Describe why this is.

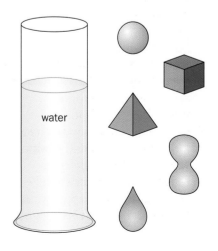

Back in the 1600s, Sir Isaac Newton investigated the way forces behaved. He found that when two objects interact, the **action** force and the **reaction** force were equal and opposite.

For instance, if a block of wood is stationary on a table, the downward force of the block (its weight) is exactly equal to the upward push of the table (the reaction).

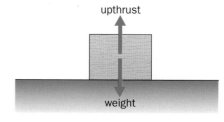

A force is a push or a pull.

You can use a pushing force to move a trolley. To just start it moving, your pushing force must just overcome the force of friction.

In a tug of war, you use a pulling force. If both teams pull with the same force, there is no movement…

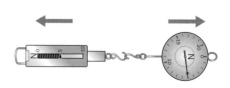

…you can check this by hooking two force meters together and pulling. What is the reading on each scale?

Weighing things in water

When you hang an object on a force meter, the reaction on the force meter equals the weight of the object. In other words, the meter measures the weight of the object.

Some pupils were experimenting and discovered something very odd. When they lowered an object into a beaker of water, the reading on the force meter got smaller. The object seemed to lose weight!

But this was not a new discovery. The Greek philosopher Archimedes noticed the same thing 2200 years ago! He suggested that the object hadn't actually lost weight, but that it was the reaction of the water that was pushing up on the object. He discovered that the amount of the upthrust was the weight of the water that had been displaced by the volume of the object.

1 A bag of sugar standing on a shelf weighs 10 N. What will be the size and direction of the reaction of the shelf? ▲
2 Make a list of machines which are designed to produce pushing or pulling forces.
3 If a metal block was weighed in air, and then weighed in water, what would happen to the reading on the force meter? Explain why this happens. ▲
4 If a wooden block was weighed in air and then weighed in water, what would happen to the reading on the force meter? Explain why this happens. What could you say about the weight of the block and upthrust of the water in this case? ▲
5 Why is it possible for a ship made of metal to float?
6 **Try to find out** why upthrust is important to a whale, and why a whale gets into serious trouble when it is beached.

DiD YOU KNOW?

◗ The story goes that Archimedes made his discovery while he was getting into a rather full bath. As the displaced water slopped over the sides he made the connection between the feeling of floating in the bath and the overflowing water.

This see-saw is very unbalanced. What will the children have to do to get it balanced?

This see-saw is nicely balanced. It looks as though both children need to be near the end.

But this child and her Dad are both near the end. And this see-saw is very unbalanced! How could this child and her Dad play on the seesaw without the child always being up in the air?

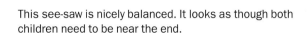

Yes, Dad has now moved towards the pivot. The see-saw is now nicely balanced. It looks as though balancing has to do with how heavy you are *and* how far away you are from the pivot point.

Working it out

People have to sit one on each side of a see-saw to make it balance. But they don't need to be the same weight. A heavy person and a light person can make the see-saw balance. But it does depend where they sit.

Look at the two see-saws on the right. Whether each see-saw balances or not depends on:

➲ **the size of the force on each side**

➲ **the distance between each force and the pivot.**

The see-saw balances when:

force × distance	=	force × distance
(on the left of the pivot)		(on the right of the pivot)

For see-saw **1**   400 N × 3 m   =   600 N × 2 m

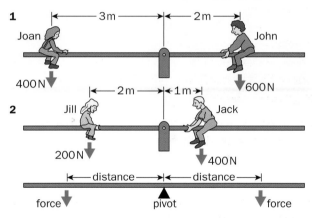

1 Balancing a see-saw depends on two things.
  a What are they?
  b What is the special relationship between them? ▲
2 Look at the see-saw pictures above.
  a Fred takes Joan's place on see-saw 1. He weighs 300 N. Where should he sit to balance? (It might help to draw a picture.)
  b Jack moves backwards on see-saw 2 until he is 1.5 m from the pivot. Where should Jill sit to keep the balance? ▲

3 If you had a plank of wood about 4 m long, and a bag of cement weighing 250 N, how could you measure the weight of one of your friends?
4 A lever works on the same principle as a see-saw. Imagine you're using a 110 cm long crowbar to lift the edge of a paving stone. If you press down with a force of 400 N, and the pivot point is 10 cm away from the stone, what force could you apply to the stone?

Balanced and unbalanced forces

On Earth, there are always forces acting on an object. When an object is stationary, or travelling at a constant speed, it is because two or more forces are balanced out.

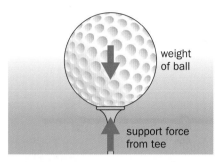

weight of ball

support force from tee

In the first picture, the weight of the golf ball is balanced by the force of the tee holding it up. The ball doesn't move.

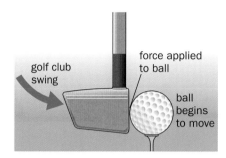

golf club swing

force applied to ball

ball begins to move

When the golf club hits, there is an unbalanced force to the right. The ball moves off to the right.

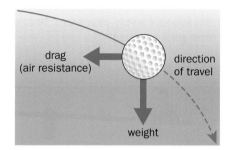

drag (air resistance)

direction of travel

weight

When a ball is in flight, gravity acts downwards, and air resistance acts to slow the ball down.

3000N
3000N
6000N

Each horse pulls with a force of 3000 N. The force pulling the plough is 6000 N. The frictional force trying to slow the plough down is 6000 N.

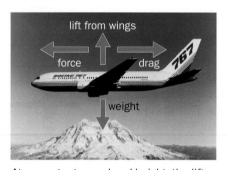

lift from wings

force   drag

weight

At a constant speed and height, the lift equals the weight, and the force from the engines equals the drag of the air.

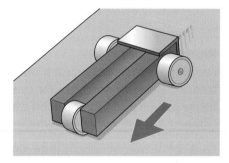

The steepness of this slope has been adjusted so that it just matches the friction on the trolley.

In the third illustration, when you apply a force to the trolley it speeds up. When you stop pulling, the trolley continues to travel at a constant speed, because the effect of the downward slope balances out the friction forces. It is as though no friction forces are acting to slow it down.

1 What happens to the speed of an object
  a when no forces act on it?
  b when all the forces acting on it balance out? ▲
2 A parachutist who weighs 800 N is falling to Earth at constant speed. What is the upwards force of the air on the parachute? ▲
3 Draw a picture of a car, with an arrow to show the force of the engine.

  a What does this force do?
  b What other forces act in a horizontal direction?
  c How do these forces affect he movement of the car?
4 You're pedalling on your bike, and you're speeding up. Make a drawing to show the forces acting in a forward and backward direction (use bigger arrows for bigger forces). Why can't you keep going faster and faster?

DiD YOU KNOW?

➲ When the engines act on a rocket in space, it changes speed or changes direction.

➲ When the engines switch off, the rocket continues to travel at a constant speed in a straight line.

➲ If no more forces act, it will continue like this for ever!

What happens if you drop a golf ball? Does it float upwards? No, of course not. It falls down, pulled by the gravitational attraction of the Earth.

The same happens with a football. As they fall, they speed up at the same rate. This speeding up is called the **gravitational acceleration**. If there was no atmosphere to produce air resistance, even a feather would accelerate at the same rate!

If you hang an object on a force meter, the upward force of the spring exactly balances the force of gravity downwards towards the centre of the Earth.

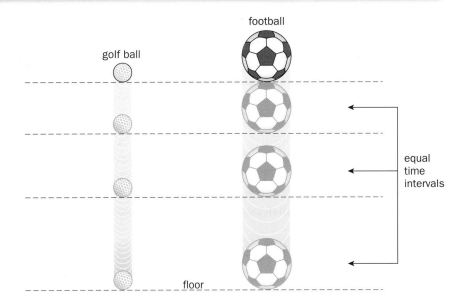

Both the light golf ball and the heavy football accelerate at the same rate due to the force of gravity.

When you hang an apple from a spring balance, the force of gravity pulls down on the apple. The spring inside the balance stretches. When you hang a bag of sugar from the same balance, the spring again stretches. Only, this time, the spring stretches further.

Why does the bag of sugar stretch the spring further? You would probably answer this by saying that the sugar is heavier than or has a larger weight than the apple.

A scientist would explain the difference by saying that the **force of gravity** pulling down on the sugar is greater than the force pulling down on the apple. In fact both these explanations agree because:

the weight of an object is the force of gravity pulling down on it.

The bigger the force of gravity pulling on an object, the bigger is its weight.

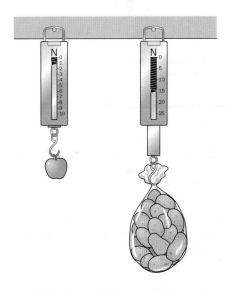

1 What is meant by the weight of an object? ▲

2 a If you dropped a ping-pong ball and a golf ball 2 m to the floor, they would both land at the same time. Why?

b If you dropped them from a high roof, the golf ball would probably land first. Explain why. ▲

3 All weighing machines do the same job. What is it? ▲

4 Does gravity pull down more on an elephant or on a mouse? Explain the reason for your answer. ▲

5 What is the force of gravity pulling down on you?

6 **Try this:** Get hold of a number of small objects (apples, oranges, books, cups, etc.). Try to judge the force of gravity acting on them and put them in order of heaviness. Now weigh them with a force meter. How good were you at judging weight?

DID YOU KNOW?

- Gravity is the name of the force that causes all objects to attract one another.

- On Earth, the gravitational force that acts between any object and the Earth is called the object's weight.

- For two 100 000 tonne ships side by side, the gravitational force of attraction between them is about 300 N.

23

Sir Isaac Newton (1642–1727) used the observations of earlier astronomers to put forward a theory to explain forces and movement. He suggested that there is a force of gravity by which *all* objects attract each other.

This gravitational force of attraction acts between any two objects. The size of the force depends on the amount of stuff in each object (its massiveness, or **mass**) and the distance between their centres.

So, the *weight* of an object on Earth (the force of gravity between it and the Earth) depends on the mass of the Earth, the mass of the object, and the distance from the centre of the Earth to the object. The **mass** of an object always remains the same, wherever it is. But the **weight** of an object at the surface of another planet will depend on the gravitational field of the planet.

This table shows the amount of gravitation acting at the surface of our Moon and the planets, compared with the Earth's **gravitational field**.

	Moon	Mercury	Venus	Earth	Mars	Jupiter	Saturn	Uranus	Neptune	Pluto
mass compared with Earth	0.01	0.06	0.82	1	0.11	317.89	95.14	14.52	17.25	0.10
diameter (km)	3500	5000	12 000	12 750	7000	140 000	120 000	52 000	50 000	5800
gravitational field compared with Earth	0.17	0.38	0.90	1	0.34	2.64	1.16	1.11	1.21	0.47

Journey to the Moon

On the Earth's surface, the astronauts weigh their normal 'Earth weight'. After take-off, as they drift farther from the Earth, their weight decreases.

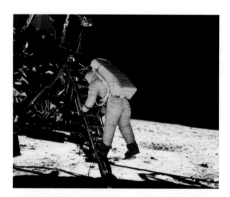

As they approach the Moon, their weight begins to increase again. After landing, the astronauts weigh one sixth of their normal weight on Earth.

DID YOU KNOW?

⮕ As the rocket motors fire and the astronauts take off, they feel very heavy. This is due to the large upward acceleration of the rocket to escape from the Earth's gravity.

⮕ If you stand on the top diving board at the swimming pool, holding a bag of potatoes from a force meter, the force meter reads zero as you fall. The potatoes, and you, have become weightless!

1 List the three things which affect the force of gravity between two objects. ▲
2 The diameters of Venus and Earth are more or less the same. Why would something weigh less on Venus than on Earth? ▲
3 Gravitational forces on the Moon are six times smaller than on Earth. What would a 600 N person weigh on the Moon?
4 **Try to measure:** the weight of various objects (in newtons) and then work out how much they would weigh on the Moon.

The box shows that scientists use the words 'mass' and 'weight' in very precise ways. And in the laboratory, you have always measured the weight of an object in newtons (N).

But in everyday life we are less precise. Go to the greengrocer and ask for 10 newtons of potatoes, and they'll not be able to help. Ask for a kilogram of potatoes and they'll understand you perfectly.

But this is OK. You know that the mass of an object does not change, but that its weight can change depending where it is. So it is perhaps good that you buy a certain **mass** of potatoes. If you went to the moon and asked for 1 kg of potatoes you'd get the same amount as at home. If you asked for 10 N of potatoes you'd get six times as many!

Measuring mass and weight

A spring stretches when a pulling force is put on it. The bigger the force, the more it stretches. This force meter has a spring inside it. The end of the spring has a pointer fixed to it. The pointer reads off on a scale marked in newtons.

You can see that there is a definite relationship between the masses hung from the force meter and the weights measured on the scale.

You can hang any object from the force meter (as long as it's not *too* heavy!) and measure its weight and work out its mass.

> **Mass** is the amount of stuff in an object. It is measured in kilograms (kg).
>
> A **force** can cause a mass to accelerate. Forces are measured in newtons (N).
>
> The **weight** of an object is the force due to gravitational attraction. Like all forces, weight is measured in newtons (N).
>
> On Earth, a mass of 1 kg weighs approximately 10 N.

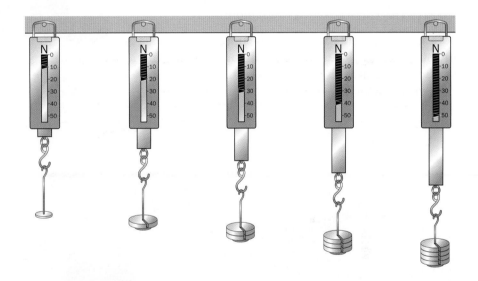

QUESTIONS

1 What is the relationship (on Earth) between the mass of an object and its weight? ▲

2 Explain how you could use a simple spring, a ruler, some standard masses and some graph paper to measure the weight of an unknown object. ▲

3 What would be the weight (on Earth) of the following masses:
   a a 25 kg bag of cement?
   b a 5 kg bag of potatoes?
   c a 1 kg bag of porridge oats?
   d a large telephone book with a mass of 1.3 kg?

e this book, with a mass of 380 g?
f a tin of treacle marked 454 g?
g a pen with a mass of 10 g?

4 Imagine you weigh a 10 kg mass in the lab, first with the type of force meter which uses a spring, and then with the type of balance which uses a pivoted beam (like a see-saw). On Earth, you would expect both machines to give a weight of 100 N. What would each machine read if you were able to repeat the measurements on the Moon? Try to explain your answer.

DID YOU KNOW?

➲ A bag of sugar with a mass of 1 kg always has the same mass.

➲ On Earth it has a weight of 10 N, on the Moon 1.7 N, on Mercury 3.8 N, on Venus 9 N, on Mars 3.4 N, and on Pluto 4.7 N.

➲ The other four planets are the gas giants and don't have a solid surface to put your bag of sugar on! But at the top of Jupiter's atmosphere, for example, the sugar would weigh 26.4 N.

Pressure is due to a force pressing on a certain area.

Hold a pencil between the palms of your hands. Now press your hands together with a *very gentle* force. Can you feel the difference? The sharp end gives a high pressure. The blunt end produces a low pressure.

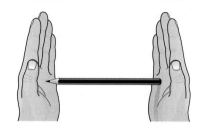

The pressure is large when the area of the surface is small.

Now press a little bit harder (but don't hurt yourself).

The pressure is larger when the force is larger.

Pressure on different surfaces

Some surfaces can withstand pressure better than others. A concrete floor can stand high pressure, but wood or vinyl floor coverings dent more easily.

Soft sand, mud, and snow will only support low pressures. Unless you take special precautions you will sink in. The layer of ice on a frozen lake will crack if the pressure is too high.

These large, low-pressure tyres spread the vehicle weight over a large area. It can travel over soft or muddy ground without sinking in.

The child, with ordinary boots, has sunk into the soft snow. But the child on the sledge stays on top.

The rescuer's weight is spread over a large area using a ladder.

Using a drawing pin

You can stick a poster on a board with a drawing pin. You push the pin with a force. The area of the point is small, so the pressure under the point is large. The point goes into the board. The area of the head is large, so the pressure against your thumb is small. It doesn't go into your thumb.

DID YOU KNOW?

➲ The legs of a *lunar module* each have a large pad at the bottom. This prevents the module sinking down in a soft or powdery surface.

1 When you are holding the pencil, which end gives the lowest pressure. ▲
2 Explain why snow shoes make it easier to walk in soft snow. ▲
3 Use the idea of pressure to explain why a sharp knife cuts better than a blunt one.
4 What is the purpose of using a ladder in a rescue on thin ice?

Observing pressure

A group of students sets out to find out more about pressure. They place blocks of different materials on a tray of sand to see how deep they sink in. They decide to do two tests:

1 with blocks of different weights resting on the same area
2 with blocks of the same weight resting on different areas.

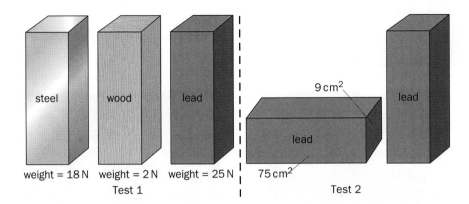

weight = 18 N   weight = 2 N   weight = 25 N
Test 1

9 cm²
lead
75 cm²
lead
Test 2

In test 1, they find that the lead block (the heaviest) sinks deepest in the sand and the wood sinks in the least. In test 2 they find that the upright block (resting on a smaller area) sinks in deepest. They conclude that pressure is largest: when the force is large, and when the area of the surface is small.

Calculating pressure To work out the pressure when a force presses on a surface you need to know two things:

➲ the size of the force (measured in newtons)
➲ the area it is pressing on (measured in square metres)

$$\text{Pressure} = \frac{\text{force}}{\text{area}} \quad \text{Its units are} \quad \frac{\text{N}}{\text{m}^2} \quad \text{or N/m}^2$$

In the lab, it is sometimes easier to measure small areas in square centimetres. This gives a pressure in N/cm².

Measuring pressure The students then weigh each block and measure the length of the sides to work out the surface area of each face. The blocks measure 3 cm, 3 cm, and 25 cm. They made their calculations using the formula above. The first one is shown for you:

$$\text{For the steel block, pressure} = \frac{\text{force}}{\text{area}} = \frac{18}{9} = 2 \text{ N/cm}^2$$

On skis, the weight of the skier is spread over a large area. This puts a smaller pressure on the snow and the skier doesn't sink in.

1 For the experiment above, calculate the pressures for
   a the wood block on its end
   b the lead block on its end
   c the lead block on its side.
   Do these values match the students' observations of how the sand was dented? ▲
2 Weigh yourself in newtons. Estimate the area of your hands, your feet, your tip-toes and the area of your back and legs when lying down. Work out the pressure you exert on the floor when you
   a stand on your hands
   b stand on one foot
   c stand on tip-toe
   d lie down.
   What are the largest and smallest of these pressures?

A fully grown camel might weigh 6000 N. The area of each of its feet is around 200 cm². These large feet reduce the pressure on the sand to prevent it sinking in.

This lady weighs 550 N. The area of each stiletto heel is 1 cm².

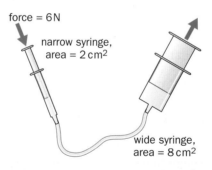

Studs on football and hockey boots stop you skidding.

This man's weight is spread over the points of thousands of nails.

Pressure in fluids

These two syringes, and the tube connecting them, are filled with a fluid.

If you push the first syringe with a force of 6 N, this produces a pressure in the fluid of 6 / 2 = 3 N.

Because the second piston has an area of 8 cm², it is pushed with a force of 3 × 8 = 24 N

The syringes have been able to magnify the force.

Systems like this can be used for car brakes and car jacks, where you apply a small force and it is converted to a larger force. Systems filled with water or oil are called **hydraulic** systems. Systems filled with gas or air are called **pneumatic** systems.

force = 6 N

narrow syringe, area = 2 cm²

wide syringe, area = 8 cm²

QUESTIONS

1 What is the pressure on the sand when a camel stands on all four feet?
2 When the lady above walks, there is one point when half her weight is on just one heel. What is the pressure under it?
3 How many times bigger is this pressure than under a camel's foot?
4 The lady's flat shoes have a heel of 10 cm². What would the pressure be under this?
5 Why do her stiletto heels dent linoleum flooring, while her flat shoes don't?
6 Work out the pressure under the studs of your boots.
7 Make lists of things that rely on
   a high pressures
   b low pressures.
8 **Try to find out** about other applications of hydraulic and pneumatic systems.

Humans and other animals have to eat food to stay alive. Food supplies the materials needed for chemical reactions in the body. It gives us energy and the building materials for us to grow. These raspberries are being harvested in Blairgowrie.

In our bodies, food is broken down into simple molecules. These are then absorbed into the body for use. This is the job of the digestive system.

The chemical energy in food is released by a process called respiration. Respiration takes place in the cells of living things and usually needs oxygen. Humans and other animals get their oxygen from the air around them. Breathing moves air into and out of the lungs. Oxygen is taken from the air and carried to the cells in the blood. Carbon dioxide is a waste product of respiration. It is carried in the blood from the cells to the lungs where it is put into the air that is breathed out.

You wouldn't expect a car to run without any fuel. The fuel supplies the energy to make the car go. Your body also needs fuel to keep it working. Its fuel is the food you eat.

But the car needs more than fuel to keep it running properly. It needs acid for its battery, water for its radiator, oil for its engine, and grease for its wheels. Your body also needs more than an energy supply. In fact, it needs a number of different chemical substances to keep it working properly. These include carbohydrates, fats, proteins, minerals, and vitamins, all of which are found in food.

Carbohydrates are important energy-supplying chemicals. The energy is released when the carbohydrates are used up in the body's cells. If you eat too much carbohydrate, your body changes it to fat.

Fats can also be used by the cells to produce energy. They can be stored in the body till needed.

Proteins are chemicals which your body needs to build up new cells and tissues.

Minerals are needed in small amounts. Different minerals are needed for different jobs. Iron is needed to make an important chemical in blood cells, while calcium and phosphorus help to make teeth.

Vitamins help to control many of the chemical changes in the body. There are thirteen different vitamins in all. The body needs only tiny amounts of each.

We also need lots of water because all the chemical reactions in the body take place in solution.

You probably get most of your energy from carbohydrates.

An Inuit gets much of their energy from fat.

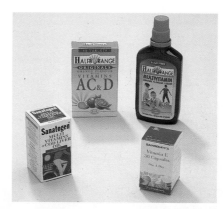
You *can* buy pills and mixtures with vitamins and minerals in them…

…but if you eat a good mixture of foods you should get all the vitamins and minerals you need.

> **DID YOU KNOW?**
> ➲ An important part of our diet is not digested. This is called **roughage**. This is mainly the cellulose walls of plant cells. It helps retain water keeping the faeces soft. It also gives the intestine muscles something to push on, keeping the food moving though the system.

1 Why does the body need:
  a carbohydrate
  b protein
  c vitamins
  d roughage? ▲

2 a What happens if you eat more carbohydrate than your body needs?
  b What happens if you eat less? ▲

3 a Why do you need lots of protein when you are growing?
  b Work out why the body needs protein to heal a cut.

4 Suggest why young children should have plenty of calcium in the food they eat.

5 **Try to find out** where the body stores fat.

The chemicals in our food are taken to the cells by the blood system. They are carried in solution in the blood **plasma**. Plasma is the liquid part of the blood.

Very small blood vessels called **capillaries** lie close to every cell in the body. The walls of capillaries are very thin with tiny holes in them. A liquid called **tissue fluid** leaks out through the holes. Tissue fluid is mainly water. It makes a continuous link between the blood plasma and the water in the cells.

Tissue fluid carries oxygen and chemicals from our food, in solution, from the blood to the cells. Wastes such as carbon dioxide travel in the opposite direction. They dissolve in the tissue fluid, which carries them to the blood.

Tissue fluid is mainly water. This is why fresh meat always looks (and feels) wet.

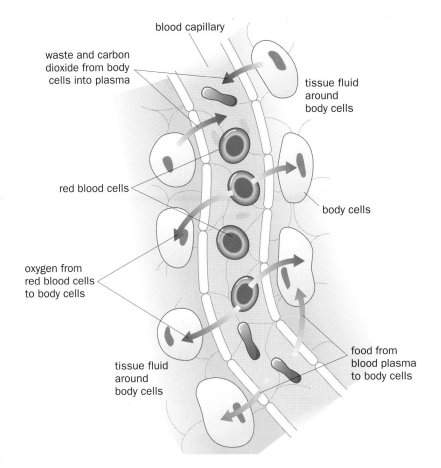

blood capillary

waste and carbon dioxide from body cells into plasma

tissue fluid around body cells

red blood cells

body cells

oxygen from red blood cells to body cells

tissue fluid around body cells

food from blood plasma to body cells

1 How are the chemicals in our food carried round the body? ▲
2 What is
  a blood plasma
  b a capillary
  c tissue fluid? ▲
3 Explain why fresh meat is wet. ▲
4 Describe how a molecule of glucose gets from the digestive system to a heart muscle cell.
5 **Try to find out** what other chemicals are carried round the body in the blood plasma.

DiD YOU KNOW?
➲ Blood capillaries are so small that in the heart, a molecule of glucose only has to travel 1/1000th of a millimetre to get to the part of the muscle cells where it is needed.

Food has to be broken down into small pieces before your body can use it. You can't swallow an apple whole! To eat the apple (or any large piece of food), you first have to bite off a piece of it. Then you have to chew the piece until it has been ground down enough for easy swallowing. Muscles, jaws, and teeth all play a part in this breakdown of the food. The muscles supply the movement. They pull on the jaws and keep them moving. Since the teeth are firmly fixed in the jaws, this keeps the teeth moving, biting, and grinding.

When an adult laughs, this is what you should see – a set of 32 gleaming white teeth. (Your smile will be less toothy! You can't expect to have 32 teeth until you are about 18).

Each jaw has 16 teeth in it. The front 4 are sharp biting teeth, called **incisors**. Behind them are 2 **canine** teeth also used for biting. The other 10 'back' teeth are much flatter. Their job is to grind the food into tiny bits. Four of these are **premolars**. The other six are **molars**.

The part of the tooth which you can see is covered by a layer of white **enamel**. This is a very hard, non-living substance. It protects the tooth and prevents it from being worn away.

The enamel covers a living part of the tooth which is made of **dentine**. The dentine is softer than enamel and is a bit like bone. In the centre of each tooth is the **pulp cavity**. This is made of soft pulp, which is made up of living cells. It also contains nerves and blood vessels.

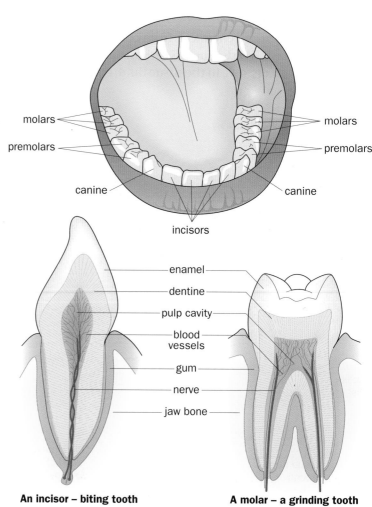

An incisor – biting tooth

A molar – a grinding tooth

1 What part do:
   a teeth
   b jaws
   c muscles play in breaking down food? ▲
2 What job is carried out by:
   a the incisors
   b the molars? ▲
3 What is:
   a dentine

   b enamel? ▲
4 The enamel protects the tooth. Why is it suitable for this?
5 How many incisors, canines, and molars do you have in each jaw? (Ask a friend to help if you find it difficult to count!)
6 **Try to find out** why canine teeth got their name.

DID YOU KNOW?
➲ Enamel is the hardest substance in the human body, yet it is affected by weak acids such as lemon juice.

The story of an adult tooth always begins in the same way. The tooth grows in the jaw underneath the gum. As it grows, it is gradually pushed towards the surface. By the time this happens, the baby teeth are well worn down. Their roots get smaller and smaller until each baby tooth falls out. Then the adult tooth pushes through to fill the gap.

How the story ends for your teeth depends on you! It can have a sad ending, or a happy one.

If you don't take care, your teeth will come to a sticky end!

New teeth grow in the jaw. When they are big enough they push through

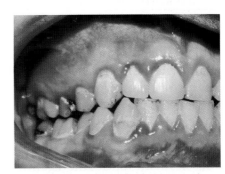

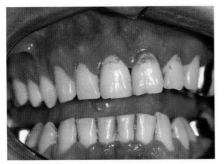

1 When you eat a food, a sticky substance called **plaque** forms on your teeth. Plaque has bacteria in it. If you eat sweet food, lots of bacteria grow.

Decay spreads through the tooth
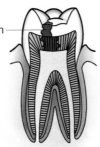

2 The bacteria change sugary food to acid. The more sweets you eat, the more acid is made. The acid eats through the enamel, making a hole. Decay starts to spread.

3 The bacteria also get into the tiny gap between teeth and gums. In this warm, wet place they multiply quickly causing disease.

1 If you cut down on sweet food, less plaque will form. If you brush your teeth well, much of the plaque which does form will be brushed away.

2 If you visit your dentist regularly she will keep a close check on your teeth and gums. She will fill holes as soon as they appear and look out for signs of gum disease.

3 Then your smile at 40 won't be very different from your smile at 14! And you won't have to keep your teeth in a glass overnight!

1 How old were you when you lost your first 'baby' tooth? Which tooth was it? Why did it fall out?
2 a What is plaque, and how does it form? ▲
  b Why does plaque cause problems for your teeth? ▲
3 a Give some good reasons for going to the dentist regularly.

  b When did you last go to the dentist? What did he (or she) do?
4 You can't feel enamel decaying. Suggest why not.
5 Make a poster with some rules about caring for your teeth.
6 **Try to find out** about fluoridation of drinking water.

DID YOU KNOW?
➲ Fluoride toothpaste helps to prevent tooth decay. Fluoride hardens the enamel.
➲ False teeth have been used since 1000 BC. The ancient Greeks used to tie them to their good teeth using strings and wires.

Food has to get into the blood to be carried to the body's cells. Only **soluble** food (food which dissolves) can do this.

Most of the food you eat, however, is **insoluble**. Even if you grind it down finely, it still won't dissolve. And so, to make use of it, your body has to break it down into chemicals which can dissolve. This breakdown is called **digestion**. It takes place in the **digestive system**.

Breaking down the food is the job of your **digestive juices**. The breakdown of some food starts in your mouth. There the food is mixed with a juice called **saliva** which is made in your **salivary glands**. As the food passes through the digestive system, other juices are added from, for example, the **liver** and the **pancreas**. Further breakdown of the food takes place.

Muscles in the walls of the digestive system keep the food moving, mixing the food and digestive juices. This speeds up digestion.

When the food has been completely broken down, it is **absorbed** into the blood. This happens in the small intestine. The small intestine has thin walls and a good blood supply to allow food to pass easily into the blood.

Some of the food you eat can't be digested. This semi-solid waste is stored in the **rectum** before passing out of the body through the **anus**.

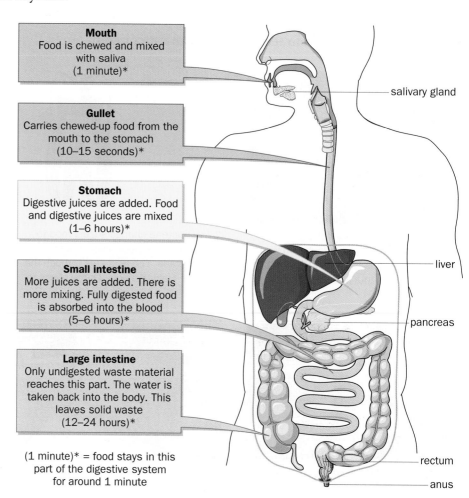

Mouth
Food is chewed and mixed with saliva
(1 minute)*

Gullet
Carries chewed-up food from the mouth to the stomach
(10–15 seconds)*

Stomach
Digestive juices are added. Food and digestive juices are mixed
(1–6 hours)*

Small intestine
More juices are added. There is more mixing. Fully digested food is absorbed into the blood
(5–6 hours)*

Large intestine
Only undigested waste material reaches this part. The water is taken back into the body. This leaves solid waste
(12–24 hours)*

salivary gland

liver

pancreas

rectum

anus

(1 minute)* = food stays in this part of the digestive system for around 1 minute

1 What happens to food in digestion? Why is this important? ▲
2 What job is done by digestive juices? Where are they made? ▲
3 What part do muscles play in digestion? ▲
4 a Bread is mostly made up of carbohydrate. If you ate toast for breakfast, where could the carbohydrate be now?
   b Some of the carbohydrate will be used by cells in your feet. Describe how it gets from your mouth to your feet.
5 a What happens to fully digested food in the small intestine? ▲
   b **Try to find out** why the wall of the intestine allows this to happen easily.

DID YOU KNOW?
➲ Chewing does matter! Finely ground food is digested more quickly than large lumps.
➲ Carbohydrates spend the shortest time in the stomach. Fats spend the longest.
➲ An adult's digestive system is about 10 m long.

Glucose and starch are two carbohydrates. They are both made up of molecules, but the molecules are very different. Glucose molecules are small . . . small enough to dissolve, and small enough to get through the wall of the intestine. And so, when you eat a glucose tablet, you don't have to digest it. The glucose dissolves in your mouth. When it reaches your intestine, it is quickly absorbed into the blood.

When you eat a starchy roll, however, it's a different story. Compared with glucose molecules, starch molecules are huge. They are far too big to dissolve, and far too big to get through the intestine wall. And so starch has to be digested before your body can use it.

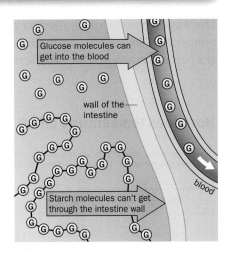

Glucose molecules can get into the blood

wall of the intestine

Starch molecules can't get through the intestine wall

blood

Enzymes at work
How does digestion change starch?

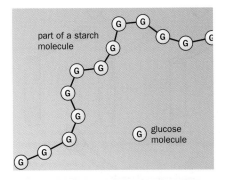

part of a starch molecule

glucose molecule

1 A starch molecule is really made up of glucose. It's a long chain made of many glucose molecules joined together.

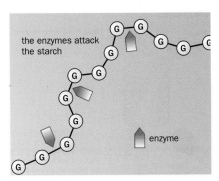

the enzymes attack the starch

enzyme

2 Digestive juices contain chemicals called **enzymes**. Some of these enzymes can attack the starch chain and can split it.

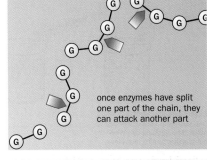

once enzymes have split one part of the chain, they can attack another part

3 When the digestive juices are mixed with starch, the starch is broken down to glucose. This glucose can then be absorbed into the blood.

The same kind of thing happens when proteins and fats are digested. Both of these chemicals are made up of large molecules which can't get through the intestine wall. Both can be broken down, by enzymes, into smaller molecules. When your food is churning around in your stomach, and intestine, the enzymes are hard at work. They're breaking up molecules.

1 Glucose molecules don't have to be digested. Starch molecules do. Explain the difference. ▲
2 What are digestive enzymes? What do they do? ▲
3 What happens to starch when it is digested? ▲
4 Saliva only contains one enzyme. That enzyme breaks down starch.

Suggest why:
a Bread begins to taste sweet when you chew it for a long time.
b The digestion of meat does not start in the mouth.
5 **Try to find out** why biological washing powders contain enzymes.

13.3 A closer look at enzymes

For the enthusiast

The way enzymes work is affected by changes in temperature and acidity (pH). Each enzyme works best at a particular temperature and level of pH.

Amylase is an enzyme found in the mouth – it is in saliva. Amylase helps in the digestion of starch into glucose. We can find out how quickly amylase breaks down starch at different temperatures and levels of pH by doing some simple experiments.

How does temperature affect enzymes?

1 A pair of test tubes, one with 1 cm³ of saliva and one 10 cm³ of starch solution is put...
...in a beaker of ice... ...in a beaker of water at 37 °C... ...in a beaker of boiling water

2 After 5 minutes the saliva and starch solutions in each beaker are mixed together.

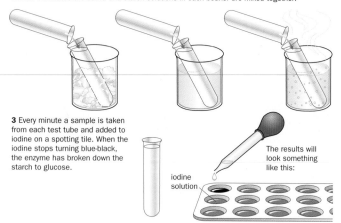

3 Every minute a sample is taken from each test tube and added to iodine on a spotting tile. When the iodine stops turning blue-black, the enzyme has broken down the starch to glucose.

iodine solution

The results will look something like this:

How does pH affect enzymes?

1 10 cm³ of starch solution is put into three test tubes. Acid (pH4) is added to one test tube... ...pure water (pH7) to the second test tube... ...and alkali (pH11) to the third test tube.

ACID   ALKALI

2 1 cm³ of saliva is added to each of the test tubes

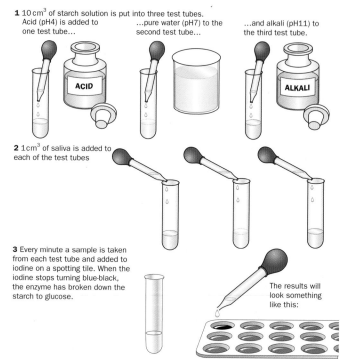

3 Every minute a sample is taken from each test tube and added to iodine on a spotting tile. When the iodine stops turning blue-black, the enzyme has broken down the starch to glucose.

The results will look something like this:

Temperature of water	Colour of iodine solution at (time/mins)									
	1	2	3	4	5	6	7	8	9	10
0 °C	●	●	●	●	●	●	●	●	●	●
37 °C	●	●	●	●	●	●	●	●	●	●
100 °C	●	●	●	●	●	●	●	●	●	●

pH of solution	Colour of iodine solution at (time/mins)									
	1	2	3	4	5	6	7	8	9	10
pH4	●	●	●	●	●	●	●	●	●	●
pH7	●	●	●	●	●	●	●	●	●	●
pH11	●	●	●	●	●	●	●	●	●	●

1 a What is amylase?
 b What does amylase do to starch?
2 Why is saliva used in these experiments?
3 Why is it important to use the same amount of saliva and starch solution in these experiments?

4 Why did each of the solutions turn iodine blue/black at the start of the experiments?
5 How can you tell how quickly the saliva digested the starch?
6 **Try to find out** the names of some other enzymes and what they do.

DID YOU KNOW?

➲ Pepsin is an enzyme that digests protein. It is part of the digestive juices made in the stomach. The digestive juices are very acidic – about pH2 – so pepsin works best in these conditions.

Breathing is simply a way of getting oxygen into the body and carbon dioxide out of it. This happens in the lungs. Blood carries oxygen from the lungs to the cells and carbon dioxide from the cells back to the lungs.

**When you breathe in, you take fresh air into the lungs.
Your body gets rid of carbon dioxide when you breathe out**

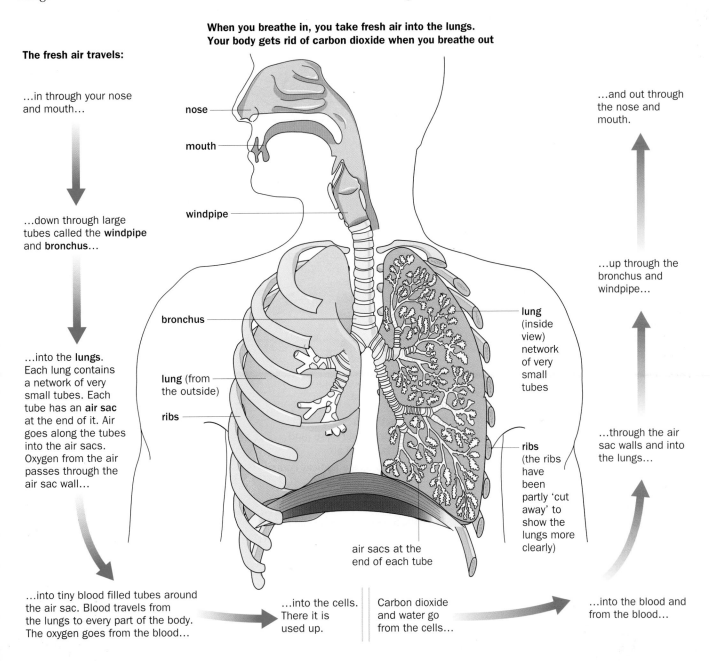

The fresh air travels:

...in through your nose and mouth...

...down through large tubes called the **windpipe** and **bronchus**...

...into the **lungs**. Each lung contains a network of very small tubes. Each tube has an **air sac** at the end of it. Air goes along the tubes into the air sacs. Oxygen from the air passes through the air sac wall...

...into tiny blood filled tubes around the air sac. Blood travels from the lungs to every part of the body. The oxygen goes from the blood...

...into the cells. There it is used up.

Carbon dioxide and water go from the cells...

...and out through the nose and mouth.

...up through the bronchus and windpipe...

...through the air sac walls and into the lungs...

...into the blood and from the blood...

nose

mouth

windpipe

bronchus

lung (from the outside)

ribs

lung (inside view) network of very small tubes

ribs (the ribs have been partly 'cut away' to show the lungs more clearly)

air sacs at the end of each tube

1 What is breathing? ▲
2 How do gases travel between the lungs and the body cells? ▲
3 Where does fresh air enter the body? ▲
4 Name the tubes that carry air into the lungs. ▲
5 Describe the inside of a lung.
6 **Try to find out** how much air a healthy person breathes in and out of their lungs.

DID YOU KNOW?
➲ There are more than 2000 km of blood vessels in your lungs.
➲ The air sac walls are only one cell thick.

1 The windpipe is a bendy tube. It has to bend when you move your head. It has rings of stiff **cartilage** (gristle) in it. These rings allow the windpipe to bend, but still keep it in a tube shape. They make sure that it doesn't close up when it bends.

2 The outside surface of the lungs is smooth and moist. This prevents the lungs from rubbing on the chest wall during breathing. The walls of the lungs cannot move themselves, but they are elastic. And so the lungs can stretch and shrink as air flows in and out.

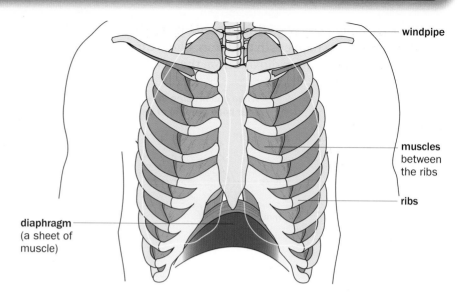

windpipe

muscles between the ribs

ribs

diaphragm (a sheet of muscle)

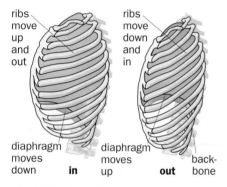

ribs move up and out

ribs move down and in

diaphragm moves down **in**

diaphragm moves up **out**

back-bone

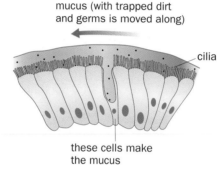

mucus (with trapped dirt and germs is moved along)

cilia

these cells make the mucus

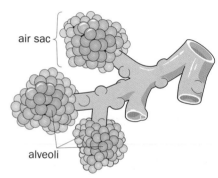

air sac

alveoli

3 Breathing in and out
Two sets of muscles control your breathing. They are the **diaphragm** and the muscles joined to the ribs. When you breathe in, the muscles tighten. This makes the ribs move out and the diaphragm move down. Air flows into the lungs. When you breathe out, your muscles relax. The ribs move in, the diaphragm moves up, and air is pushed out of your lungs.

4 Cleaning up the air
Along the inside of your nose (and windpipe and bronchii) are:

➲ cells which produce a sticky liquid called **mucus**

➲ cells with moving hairs called **cilia**.

These cells help to take dirt from the air you breathe in. The mucus traps the dirt. Then the cilia move the mucus along the tubes, away from the lungs.

5 Air sacs and alveoli
There are millions of air sacs in each of your lungs. Each air sac is made up of tiny hollow bubbles called **alveoli**. And so there is a very big surface for gases to get into and out of the blood. The inside of each air sac is moist. The gas dissolves in the moisture, then passes through the air sac wall.

1 Why is it important that
  a The windpipe has rings of cartilage in it?
  b The surface of the lungs is smooth and slimy?
  c The air sacs have a large surface area? ▲
2 What are 'mucus' and 'cilia'? How do they help to clean up the air you breathe in? ▲

3 Gases can move easily between the lungs and the blood. Give two reasons for this.
4 Why are the inside walls of the alveoli moist?
5 **Try to find out** what effect smoking can have on lungs.

DID YOU KNOW?
➲ The surface area of all the air sacs put together is about the same area as a tennis court.
➲ You either swallow, or cough up, the mucus (and dirt and germs).

Breathing and producing energy go 'hand in hand'. Your body can't do one without doing the other. But they are not the same thing.

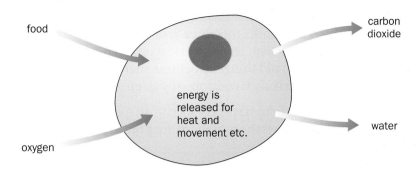

Your body gets its energy from a chemical reaction which goes on in its cells. This chemical reaction is called **respiration**. Respiration is a bit like burning. The fuel is glucose in the food we eat. The oxygen needed to 'burn' the glucose comes from the lungs. Energy (mainly heat and movement) is released. Carbon dioxide and water are produced as waste products.

Respiration can be written as this word equation:

glucose + **oxygen** → **carbon dioxide** + **water** + **ENERGY**

This means that when your cells are producing energy they:

➲ use up oxygen
➲ produce carbon dioxide and water

And so, to keep producing energy your body needs:

➲ a supply of oxygen
➲ to get rid of carbon dioxide (which could poison it)

That's where breathing comes in. You breathe in fresh air. It contains the oxygen you need. You get rid of the carbon dioxide when you breathe out stale air. It also contains water vapour.

This is how the air changes when you breathe in and out:

If you breathe on a cold window, you can see some of the water from your breath.

Gas	Amount in the air breathed in	Amount in the air breathed out
oxygen	21%	17%
carbon dioxide	0.04%	4%
nitrogen	79%	79%
water vapour	varies	saturated

DID YOU KNOW?

➲ During respiration your cells don't go on fire! The energy is released from glucose slowly and at much lower temperatures. Enzymes control respiration in cells.

You can find out how much energy is in a food by looking at the label on the packet.

1 What do living cells need to produce energy? ▲
2 a What is respiration?
  b Write a word equation for respiration. ▲
3 Why do you have to breathe to produce energy?

4 Why does a cold window steam up when you breathe on it?
5 Which of the jars shown in the diagram will
  a let a lighted splint burn longer
  b turn lime water milky?

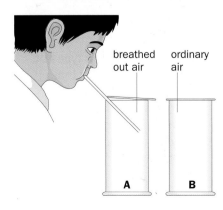

breathed out air   ordinary air

A   B

There are thousands of chemical reactions going on inside your body all the time. If your body is to work properly each of these chemical reactions needs to be carefully controlled. There are two types of chemical reaction in the body – they either build things up or break them down. Every chemical reaction in your body is controlled by an enzyme.

Enzymes are proteins. Proteins have very specific shapes which help them do their job. The shape allows the enzyme to 'lock on' to particular chemicals.

An enzyme may react with one big chemical and pull it apart, when we digest our food for example.

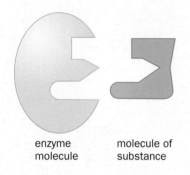

enzyme molecule   molecule of substance

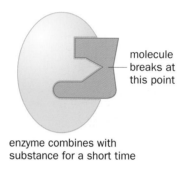

molecule breaks at this point

enzyme combines with substance for a short time

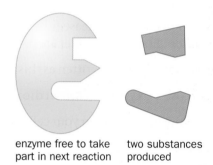

enzyme free to take part in next reaction   two substances produced

...or an enzyme may bring two chemicals together to make a bigger one, for example when we are growing and need to build new cells.

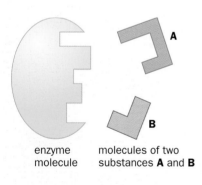

enzyme molecule   molecules of two substances **A** and **B**

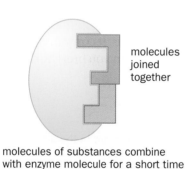

molecules joined together

molecules of substances combine with enzyme molecule for a short time

enzyme free to take part in another reaction   new substance formed

Notice how the enzymes and chemicals fit together like a key in a lock. That is why each enzyme is specific to one chemical reaction. It is called the 'lock and key theory'.

1 a What are the two types of chemical reaction that happen in your body?
b How are these chemical reactions controlled?
2 Why is the shape of an enzyme important?

3 Describe how an enzyme breaks down a food molecule.
4 How does the lock and key theory helps to explain how enzymes do their job?
5 Try to find out why enzymes are sometimes called 'biological catalysts'.

DID YOU KNOW?
➲ Biological washing powders contain enzymes which break down food, grease, or dirt stains on clothes. They only work at low temperatures though – can you think why?

The Forth rail bridge and the Forth road bridge are two amazing feats of engineering. The rail bridge is a cantilever bridge, one of the strongest ever built, while the road bridge is one of the biggest suspension bridges. Originally, the rail bridge was also going to be a suspension bridge. But, as it was being designed, the Tay bridge disaster took place. Six months after it was built, part of the Tay bridge was blown into the river during a hurricane, and a train and 70 passengers were lost. After that, public opinion demanded that the Forth bridge should be the strongest possible design. That made it one of the most expensive bridges ever!

Both bridges are built of huge steel structures on concrete bases. 50 000 tonnes of steel were used in the rail bridge and 35 000 tonnes in the road bridge. To make the steel, the iron had to be separated from iron ore in huge ironworks. Then it had to be mixed with other metals to make steel. The engineers had to choose a steel that was stronger than iron, but that also stood up to corrosion. Corrosion is a major problem for both bridges as the sea water attacks the steel and rusts it. How the iron is produced and how it is protected against corrosion are just two of the things you will learn in this chapter.

What metals have in common

You will be very familiar with some metals. Metals in everyday use include **iron** (nails), **copper** (water pipes), **tin** (on the surface of cans), **gold** and **silver** (jewellery), **aluminium** (greenhouses), and **chromium** (on bicycle handlebars). Others are more rare. You are unlikely to have seen a piece of pure palladium, for example. It's a scarce metal used in the making of margarine and crowns for teeth! But if you were to see it, you would easily recognise it as a metal, and be able to prove that it was a metal by doing simple tests. Why?

Made of gold: Jules Rimet World Cup

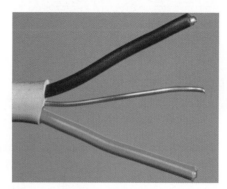
Copper cable

Aluminium being worked

All metals are shiny and reflect light

Sometimes the surface of the metal is covered with corrosion (like rust) but rubbing it off will show the shiny metal underneath. Metals which stay shiny are used for decoration, jewellery and ornaments.

All metals are good conductors of electricity

Electric current is carried through homes by copper wires, through a light bulb by tungsten wires and across country, from pylon to pylon, by cables made from aluminium.

All metals are malleable

You can change their shapes by hammering them. They won't break easily.

Metals such as aluminium are ductile

They can be drawn out into thin wires without breaking.

The only substances which can do all of these things are metals. There are some non-metals which can do one or two of these things. Many crystals, for example, are shiny and reflect light, but they don't conduct electricity. Graphite is a type of carbon which conducts electricity well, but it is brittle and breaks easily. Many plastics can be drawn out into threads and can have their shapes changed without breaking, but they don't conduct electricity. Only metals can reflect light **and** conduct electricity **and** have their shapes changed **and** be drawn out into wires without breaking.

Fool's gold has confused many gold-miners. It's iron sulphide.

1 a What are metals used for in your science lab? Make a list of the uses and name as many of the metals as you can. ▲
   b How did you pick out the metals? ▲
2 a Give three tests which you could use to pick out a metal. ▲
   b How could miners tell the difference between real gold and fool's gold?

3 How are the following like a metal? How are they different?
   a diamond
   b graphite
   c polythene.
4 Cars dent in accidents but don't break. Why is this useful?
5 **Try to find out:**
   a which metals are magnetic
   b what metal detectors are used for
   c how mirrors are made.

DID YOU KNOW?

➲ The reflecting surface in a mirror is a very thin layer of silver (or aluminium or tin).

➲ 29 g of gold can be drawn into a thread 100 km long.

When you put different metals in water, some react and some don't. Potassium and sodium react very fast, giving off lots of hydrogen gas. Magnesium reacts very slowly – it would take weeks to collect enough bubbles of hydrogen to 'pop'! Most metals don't react at all.

When metals are put into hydrochloric acid, the same kind of thing happens. A few metals – **unreactive metals** – don't react with the acid. (They don't react with water either.) Some metals which didn't react with water do give off bubbles of hydrogen gas in acid. The metals which reacted with water react faster with the acid. In fact, calcium, sodium, and potassium react so violently that they should never be put in acid.

It's not so easy to compare how quickly metals react with oxygen, but the pattern is the same. Potassium, sodium, and calcium react quickly. (The freshly cut metal quickly loses its shiny surfaces as the metal reacts with the oxygen in the air.) Some metals (tin, copper, gold, silver) don't react and stay shiny. Heating a metal does make it react better with oxygen, but even strong heating won't make gold react.

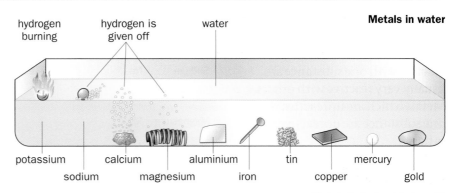

Metals in water

hydrogen burning — hydrogen is given off — water

potassium — sodium — calcium — magnesium — aluminium — iron — tin — copper — mercury — gold

Metals in hydrochloric acid

hydrogen is given off — hydrochloric acid

magnesium — aluminium — zinc — iron — tin — lead — copper — mercury — silver — gold

Magnesium burns very brightly in oxygen…

…but even strong heating won't make gold react.

QUESTIONS

1 From the diagram, pick out
  a one metal that reacts with water and acid and
  b two that react with acid only. ▲
2 a What is an unreactive metal? ▲
  b Which unreactive metals are used for making jewellery and why? ▲

3 Design a fair test to investigate whether magnesium reacts faster with water or acid. What would you expect to observe?
4 Which of the metals shown above *could* you use to make water pipes? Suggest why some of the metals are **not** used.
5 **Try to find out** what platinum is used for.

DID YOU KNOW?
➲ When potassium reacts with water, so much heat is produced that the hydrogen catches fire.
➲ Platinum is even less reactive than gold.

When you read about the reactions of metals, you probably noticed a pattern. Metals that are very reactive with one substance are usually very reactive with others. Metals which are unreactive with one substance are unreactive with others.

The **reactivity series** is a kind of league table of metals. It puts the metals in order with the fastest reacting metals first. Potassium is at the top of the table. It reacts very quickly with water. It reacts so violently with acid that it should never be put in it! Silver and gold are at the bottom of the league because they hardly react at all.

A 'league table' of reactivity

Potassium	K
Sodium	Na
?	?
Magnesium	Mg
Aluminium	Al
?	?
Iron	Fe
?	?
Lead	Pb
Copper	Cu
Silver	Ag
Gold	Au

Most reactive

Least Reactive

Using the reactivity series – displacement reactions

If an iron nail is left in a copper sulphate solution, the nail becomes red-brown. The iron atoms from the nail react and go into the solution. The copper atoms that were in the solution form a layer of red-brown solid copper on the nail.

This is a **displacement reaction**. The iron has **displaced** the copper from the solution. The reaction works because iron is higher in the reactivity series than copper. The reaction also works when magnesium, zinc, and aluminium are put in copper sulphate, but not for gold or silver. **A displacement reaction only takes place when the metal that is put into the solution is higher in the reactivity series than the metal in the solution.**

This reaction is used to get valuable copper from poor quality ores. The ores have so little copper and so much other waste material that it is not worthwhile trying to extract the copper by normal methods. By dissolving the ore and then putting scrap iron in the solution, it is possible to collect the copper on the iron.

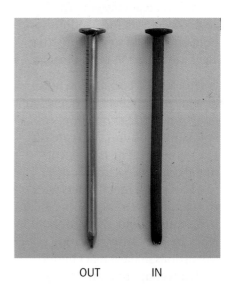

OUT   IN

1 What is the reactivity series? Why is gold at the bottom of the series? Why is potassium at the top? ▲

2 Copy out the table at the top of the page. Then use the information on the last page to put the missing metals tin, calcium, and zinc in order in the series. ▲

3 a When an iron nail is put into a copper sulphate solution, there is a displacement reaction. What happens? ▲

b Explain what would happen if silver and zinc were used instead.

4 Try to find out what nickel is like and where it should go in the reactivity series.

DID YOU KNOW?

➲ Three hundred years ago, Spanish workers were using iron to extract copper from a copper solution.

➲ Nowadays, bacteria are used to get copper from poor quality copper ore. The bacteria get energy from the ore. As they do so, they convert the copper in the ore into copper solution.

In 1848, some workmen spotted gold while digging a ditch in California. The news of their find spread like wildfire! Within a very short time, thousands and thousands of gold prospectors were heading for the area by land and sea. The great Californian gold rush was on. Everyone wanted to make a fortune, and some did.

The real finds were veins of pure gold in rocks or nuggets of pure gold in streams. The gold was found as **native metal** (a metal which is found in nature as the element.)

Only gold and a few other metals at the foot of the reactivity series are found like this. The other metals are found as compounds in **metal ores**. That's because these metals are more reactive. Some time in the past, they have reacted with elements like oxygen and sulphur to make compounds like oxides and sulphides. This is most likely to have happened in parts of the Earth where temperatures were high. Much of the iron, for example, reacted with oxygen from the air.

iron + **oxygen** → **iron oxide**
   (from   (in the
   the air)   iron ore)

In the photographs, you can see some of the main metal ores, and where they come from.

Gold prospectors…

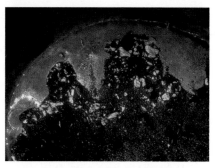
…and what they were looking for

Bauxite – ore which gives most aluminium – mainly aluminium oxide – main sources Australia, China, Brazil

Haematite – ore which gives most iron – mainly iron oxide – main sources Australia, Brazil

Copper pyrites – ore which gives most copper – mainly copper sulphide – main sources Chile, USA

Magnesium chloride – compound which gives most magnesium – found in the sea

1 a What is a 'native metal'? ▲
  b Which of the following metals would you expect to find native? Why?
     silver   zinc   sodium
     magnesium   copper
2 a What is a metal ore?
  b Why are most metals found as compounds in ores? ▲

3 Which elements are joined with
  a aluminium in bauxite
  b copper in copper pyrites? ▲
4 Why do you think there have been gold and silver rushes but no aluminium rushes?
5 Try to find out:
  a where silver and gold have been found in Scotland
  b how panning for gold works.

DID YOU KNOW?

➲ Rocks which have enough metal in them to make mining worthwhile are called **ores**.

➲ There is a little native iron on the Earth. It is contained in meteorites – lumps of rock which have crashed onto Earth from space.

A Californian gold prospector who was lucky enough to strike gold did not have difficulty getting the pure metal. All of the gold was found as native metal. It is is usually more difficult to obtain metals from their ores. Normally two steps have to be carried out. First, the metal compound is separated from the rock and other waste material. Then the metal compound has to be broken up to set the metal free.

Iron oxide and coke (carbon) are loaded in, along with limestone which takes away impurities

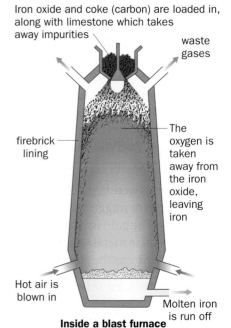

Inside a blast furnace

Smelting metal ores

Magnetite is one form of iron oxide found in iron ores. It is magnetic. Iron is produced from magnetite ore in two steps:

$$\text{iron} + \text{carbon} \rightarrow \text{iron} + \text{carbon}$$
$$\text{oxide} \qquad\qquad \text{dioxide}$$

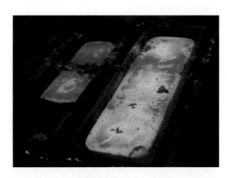

1 **The magnetite is separated from other materials in the ore.** The ore is crushed to powder and mixed with water in separating tanks. The magnetite is separated using magnets which attract the magnetic iron oxide, leaving the rest of the rock.

2 **The iron oxide is smelted.** In smelting, a metal ore is heated so that the metal can be separated from it. In this case, the iron oxide is heated with carbon in a blast furnace. The oxygen is removed from the iron oxide, leaving iron.

Tin, lead, and copper can also be obtained by smelting their compounds with carbon. But aluminium, magnesium, and sodium compounds can't be smelted in this way. The metal compounds are melted, then an electric current is passed through the hot liquid producing the pure metal. This is called **electrolysis**.

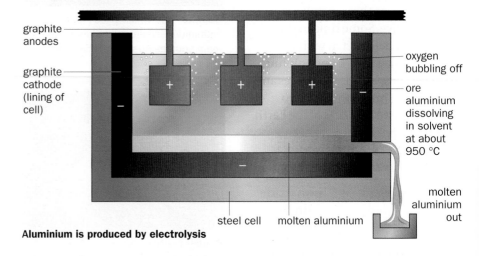

Aluminium is produced by electrolysis

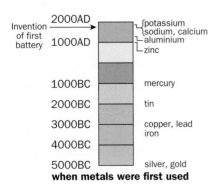

when metals were first used

1 Write down two steps carried out in smelting metal ores. ▲
2 When iron is being produced from magnetite ore
  a how is the magnetite separated from the waste materials? ▲
  b how is the iron obtained from the iron oxide ore?
3 How is aluminium produced? ▲

4 Look at the metals which are obtained by smelting their ores with carbon and the metals which need electrolysis. Is there a pattern?
5 Look at the date diagram.
  a How long ago was copper first used?
  b Which metals could Julius Caesar have used?
6 **Try to find out** why several metals were discovered around 1800 AD.

Millions of tonnes of metals are used every year for many different jobs. They are used for building cars and bridges (iron), making drink cans and food packaging (aluminium), plumbing and electrical wires (copper) and making batteries (zinc). But they all face one problem. That is **corrosion**.

A metal corrodes whenever a chemical – like water, air, or acid – attacks its surface. First, the metal loses its shiny surface. Then it is slowly eaten away and weakened. Metals at the top of the reactivity series can't be used to make things because they are quickly corroded by water and air. But corrosion is even a problem for metals lower in the series. Corrosion of cars and bridges made of steel (which is mainly iron) can weaken them and make them dangerous to use. Corrosion is also expensive! Replacing corroded metal objects costs hundreds of millions of pounds every year.

Corrosion (rusting) of cars makes them dangerous to use.

Using protective coatings

One good way to prevent a metal from corrosion is to give it a coating which protects it against water and air. Paint can be used. So can grease and oil (for moving metal parts). A coating of an unreactive metal can do the same job. Tin cans, for example, are made of steel (which makes them strong and cheap) and coated with tin (to protect the steel from being corroded by the food in the can).

Some protective coatings can be put on by **electroplating**. The photograph shows how electroplating is done. The item to be electroplated is connected to the negative of a power supply, then put in a solution containing a metal compound. The electricity breaks up the compound. The metal atoms in the solution move to the 'item' and a layer of metal is formed on the surface.

1 What makes a metal corrode? ▲ What happens when it corrodes? ▲
2 Why is corrosion a problem
   a for a bridge
   b for a cycle chain? ▲
3 Write down 3 ways of preventing corrosion. Which would you use to protect
   a an iron fence
   b steel bicycle handlebars
   c a cycle chain? ▲
4 Why does a tin can have more than one metal in it? ▲
5 Some car door handles are covered with shiny chromium. It is added by electroplating. Using the silver plated cutlery example above, suggest how this could be done. ▲

DID YOU KNOW?

➲ Iron won't corrode in water – as long as there is no oxygen dissolved in it.

➲ A car body can be protected against corrosion by connecting it to the negative terminal of the car battery.

When you have finished using a metal object, like a rusty bicycle or an empty drinks can, you have two options. You can throw it away, or you can **recycle** it.

Recycling means using waste materials to make new ones. It's by far the better option for the following reasons:

aluminium	30 yrs
iron	320 yrs
gold	30 yrs
copper	70 yrs
lead	50 yrs
tin	40 yrs

1. Recycling protects the countryside.
Thrown-away rubbish has to be put somewhere. More and more land is being used for tips, and they don't do much for the countryside!

2. Recycling saves the world's metals.
The world's metal supplies won't last for ever. The diagram gives estimates of how long the ore supplies will last for some of the most used metals.

3. Recycling saves the world's energy.
It takes far less energy to manufacture something from recycled metal than from metal obtained from an ore.

What should we do?

We have to do something – Britain has one of the worst records in Western Europe for recycling!

We could start by recycling aluminium drink cans in school. At home, we can encourage everyone to recycle plastic bottles, glass bottles, scrap metal, paper, and cardboard.

	steel	aluminium	glass
Austria	70%	50%	65%
France	47%	19%	55%
Germany	81%	86%	81%
Netherlands	71%	66%	84%
Sweden	71%	87%	84%
Switzerland	63%	89%	91%
Great Britain	25%	38%	24%

The amounts recycled in different countries in 1998

1 What is meant by recycling? ▲
2 Give 3 reasons why recycling is important. ▲
3 Which metal ores are most likely
   a to run out first
   b to last longest? ▲
4 Explain why recycling helps to cut down on the amount of energy used. ▲

5 Draw a bar graph to show how much steel is recycled by the countries in the table. Then do the same for
   a aluminium
   b glass. ▲
6 **Try to find out** where your nearest recycling centre is, and what it recycles. Then try to persuade people to use it.

DID YOU KNOW?

➲ It takes 20 times more energy to make a can from aluminium ore than from recycled aluminium.

➲ We use 7 billion aluminium cans each year in Britain, five times more than the next biggest European user, Italy.

Unreactive metals can be used to solve some corrosion problems, but not all. For one thing, most unreactive metals are expensive. For another, they are often unsuitable for the job. Even if gold was cheap and plentiful, it wouldn't be used for bridge building! It's far too soft and weak for that.

Most corrosion problems are solved using **metal alloys**. An alloy is a mixture of two or more metals. Alloys are usually made by melting metals together, then allowing the molten mixture to cool and harden. Mixing different metals can produce alloys which behave in different ways. Many of the alloys are designed to be corrosion resistant.

Many alloys belong to the family of **steels**. The main metal in steel is iron, but iron rusts easily and is quite brittle. Alloying the iron with metals like nickel and chromium, however, makes steels which are stronger and rust-resistant.

In the pictures you can see alloys, the main metals in them and some of the jobs they do. *All of them have been designed to be corrosion resistant.*

Duralumin
Aluminium (95%), copper (4%)
hard, strong, lightweight.
Used in aircraft manufacture.

Monel
Nickel (70%), copper (30%)
strong, unaffected by sea water.
Used in shipbuilding e.g. propellers.

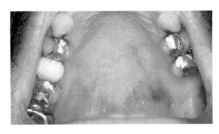

Amalcap
Tin (44%), mercury (33%), silver (23%)
unaffected by mouth acids, sets hard.
Used to make fillings in teeth.

Stainless steel
Iron (85%), chromium (15%)
strong, corrosion resistant.
Used to make cutlery, jewellery.

Solder
Lead (66%), tin (33%)
melts at a low temperature, then sets hard. Used to make metal connections.

Iconel
Nickel (70%), chromium (17%)
Strong, unaffected by high temperature.
Used in rocket engines.

QUESTIONS

1 What is
  a a metal alloy
  b a corrosion resistant alloy? ▲
2 How are alloys made? How is steel made? ▲
3 In what way(s) are
  a steel better than iron
  b bronze better than copper
  c amalcap better than mercury? ▲
4 Why is
  a monel a good alloy for shipbuilding

  b solder useful for electrical work
  c iconel used in rocket engines? ▲
5 One of the alloys described above is used in nuclear reactors. Another is used for racing car bodies. Using the information above, decide which is which, giving reasons. ▲
6 **Try to find out** where stainless steel is used and why.

Bronze
Copper (85%), tin (15%)
Stronger than copper.
Used to make statues.

By now you have met many different elements. This unit has been dealing with metals which make up most of the elements. They have lots of things in common – they are all shiny, good conductors, and can have their shapes changed without breaking. However, they can react quite differently. (Think of what happens when sodium and copper are put in water, or magnesium and gold are heated in air!) You have also met several non-metals, like oxygen, carbon, chlorine, and hydrogen. They are quite different from the metals and react differently.

Why are the elements so different? Why do they react in such different ways? **It's all because their atoms are different.**

All atoms* are made up of the same tiny particles

There are three types of particle
proton (p) which carries one positive charge
electron (e) which has one negative charge
neutron (n) which has no charge

The particles are so small that their masses can't be measured in grams. They are measured in
atomic mass units (AMUs)
proton mass = 1 AMU
neutron mass = 1 AMU
electron mass = 0 (so small that it can be ignored)

(* apart from hydrogen)

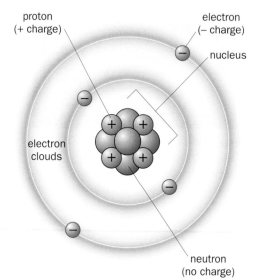

proton (+ charge)
electron (– charge)
nucleus
electron clouds
neutron (no charge)

All atoms have the same basic structure

The protons and neutrons are found in the **nucleus** at the centre of the atom. Because the protons and the neutrons make up all of the mass of the atom, and because it is tiny, the nucleus is very, very dense.

The electrons take up all the space outside the nucleus. They whiz round in **electron clouds** at an incredibly high speed (2 000 000 m/s). They move so fast that it is as if they are everywhere at the same time.

Atoms of different elements have different numbers of protons, neutrons, and electrons. The simplest atom is hydrogen. It has 1 proton and 1 electron but no neutrons. Helium has 2 protons, 2 neutrons, and 2 electrons. Here, you can see the particles in other atoms. Looking carefully, you should see that:
the number of protons in an atom is equal to the number of electrons.

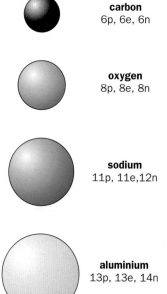

carbon
6p, 6e, 6n

oxygen
8p, 8e, 8n

sodium
11p, 11e,12n

aluminium
13p, 13e, 14n

1 a What are the three tiny particles which make up atoms? ▲
  b Write down the charge and mass of each one. ▲
2 What is the nucleus? What does it contain? ▲
3 Where are electrons found in an atom? They are tiny, but take up most of the atom's space. How can they do that? ▲
4 In what way is hydrogen different from the other atoms?
5 **Try to find out** the elements whose atoms have:
  a 17 protons
  b 7 electrons
  c 20 neutrons

With over 100 elements each with different numbers of protons, electrons, and neutrons, scientists found it helpful to make an 'atomic shorthand'. They now use **atomic numbers** and **mass numbers** to describe atoms.

⮑ **The atomic number of an element is the number of protons an atom of the element has in the nucleus.** (It is also equal to the number of electrons in the atom.)

⮑ **The mass number is equal to the number of protons plus the number of neutrons.** (The electrons don't count because their mass is so small.)

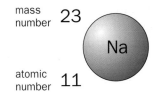

mass number 23

atomic number 11

The 'atomic shorthand' for some common elements

oxygen: $^{16}_{8}O$ copper: $^{64}_{29}Cu$ gold: $^{197}_{79}Au$ silver: $^{108}_{47}Ag$

carbon: $^{12}_{6}C$ chlorine: $^{35}_{17}Cl$ iron: $^{56}_{26}Fe$ sodium: $^{23}_{11}Na$

Electrons in an atom

In an atom, electrons are considered to be in energy levels, or **shells**. Electrons in the first shell are nearer to the nucleus and have lower energy than those in the second shell. The electrons in the second shell are nearer the nucleus and have lower energy than those in the third shell and so on.

Electrons in an atom always go into the lowest possible shell, but each shell can only take a certain number of electrons before it is full up. The first shell is full after it has 2 electrons in it, the second is full when it has 8. Once a shell is full, any extra electrons have to go into the next shell.

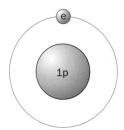

Hydrogen (1e)

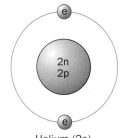

Helium (2e)

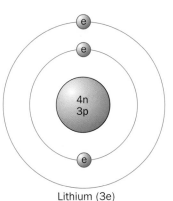

Lithium (3e)

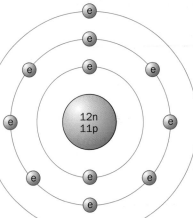

Sodium (11e)

1 What is
  a the atomic number
  b the mass number of an element? ▲
2 How can you use the atomic number and the mass number to find the number of protons, electrons, and neutrons in an atom? ▲
3 Write down the numbers of protons, neutrons, and electrons in the atoms whose 'atomic shorthand' is given above. ▲
4 Electrons move around the nucleus in energy levels or shells. What is the difference between electrons in the 1st and 2nd shells? ▲
5 **Try to find out** the name for the elements which have full outer shells of electrons.

DiD YOU KNOW?

⮑ You can work out the number of p, e, and n in an atom from the atomic number and mass number:

No of p = atomic number

No of e = atomic number

No of n = mass number – atomic number

The last two pages have given you a very simple picture of what the atom is like. It's far more complicated than that! Scientists took over 100 years to work out the structure you have been given, and work is still going on. Here are some of the scientists who made important discoveries about the atom – and their 'big ideas'.

John Dalton, a British scientist who was a teacher in Manchester, was the first scientist to work out that everything was made of atoms (1808). His first ideas came from studying the weather. He decided that water could only evaporate into the air if water and air were made up of particles which could mix through each other. He then had the idea that everything was made up of particles called atoms which could not be broken down into simpler particles. He thought that different atoms would have different weights and did experiments to prove it.

Joseph John (JJ) Thomson (1897) had the big idea that there were particles which were smaller than an atom. Investigating the rays from a cathode ray tube (like the tube of a TV) he found that the rays were made of tiny negative particles, smaller than an atom. These particles were later called **electrons**. In his model of the atom, most of the space was taken up by positively charged material, with many tiny electrons spread through it – like the currents in a current bun!

Ernest Rutherford: The next idea arose from a set of experiments carried out in 1911. When a beam of positive particles was fired at very thin gold foil, most particles went straight through but a very few were repelled straight back. Since positive particles can only be repelled by something positive, this suggested to Rutherford that:

1 there must be a positive part at the centre of each atom
2 it must be very small (since most particles went straight through)

His model of the atom had a tiny positive **nucleus** and most of the atom as empty space with electrons whizzing round in it.

Neils Bohr did some complicated calculations in 1922 that showed there were only a few energy levels or shells which the electrons could go into. This discovery helped to explain the periodic table.

John Dalton

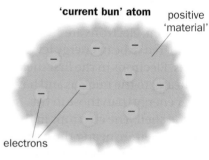

JJ Thomson's model

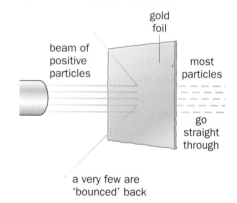

QUESTIONS

1 What were Dalton's big ideas? Which of the ideas do we still use today? ▲
2 a What did JJ Thomson discover? ▲
  b Why was his model of the atom called the 'current bun' model? ▲

3 What happens when positive particles are fired at thin gold foil? Why does this happen?
4 What was Rutherford's model of the atom? Do we still use it?

DID YOU KNOW?

➲ The experiments in which the positive particles were repelled back off the gold foil really surprised Rutherford. He said it was as if a shell fired by a battleship had bounced back off a sheet of paper.

➲ Dalton was the first person to recognise colour blindness!

Group	①	②							③	④	⑤	⑥	⑦	⑧	←
Row ①														He 2	No. of electrons in outer shell
②	Li 3	Be 4							B 5	C 6	N 7	O 8	F 9	Ne 10	
③	Na 11	Mg 12							Al 13	Si 14	P 15	S 16	Cl 17	Ar 20	
④	K 19	Ca 20	Sc 21	Ti 22			Cu 29	Zn 30	Ga 31	Ge 32	As 33	Se 34	Br 35	Kr 36	

H 1

You may find it difficult to understand the periodic table but understanding this part is very difficult. That's why we leave it alone.

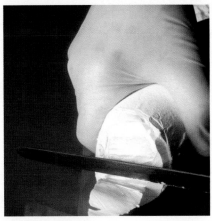

Alkali metals All have 1 e in the outer shell. All are soft metal, can be cut with a knife and are very reactive with water and air.

Knowing about **atomic number**, and about electrons in their shells, helps you to understand the periodic table better. The table has **rows** (across) and **groups** (down each column). Each of the elements has its atomic number written beside it. If you follow the elements across a row in the table, you will see that the atomic number goes up by one. The elements in the table are arranged **in order of increasing atomic number**.

Electron arrangements

The electron arrangements in the atoms explain why a new row starts when it does. Whenever an electron shell has 8 electrons in it (or 2 electrons in the case of helium), it is full. If another electron has to be added, it will have to go into the next shell. This means that every element in group 8 has 8 electrons in its highest electron shell, every element in group 1 has 1 electron in the outer shell and so on.

The number of electrons in the outer shell of its atom has a big effect on the way an element reacts. That's why elements in the same group of the table tend to react in the same way.

The most famous chemical family is the set of noble gases. They are famous because they don't react! They all have full outer shells of 8 electrons or 2 in the case of helium. *Because they have full outer shells, they don't react.*

The alkali metals and the halogens are two other chemical families. Here, you can see what they are like – and why they are similar.

Halogens All have 7 e in the outer shell. All are coloured, poisonous, non-metals and are very reactive.

1 Copy and complete
   In the periodic table of elements, the elements are arranged _____ across a row. All the elements in a group have _____. A new group is started _____ ▲

2 How many electrons do
   a nitrogen
   b germanium
   c calcium have in the outer shell? How did you get your answer? ▲

3 Why do
   a the noble gases
   b the alkali metals each make a chemical family? What do the elements in each family have in common?

4 **Try to find out:**
   a what the word 'noble' means
   b why the noble gases have been well named
   c where the coinage metals are in the table.

DID YOU KNOW?

⊃ Copper, silver, and gold make up a chemical family called the coinage metals. They are all unreactive, don't corrode and, as a result have been used to make coins.
Guess what? They are all in the same column in the periodic table!

Light and sound

No one can see anything in a completely darkened room. There has to be light before you can see. You see when light enters your eye. Light is a kind of energy. Light energy is given off by the Sun, by electric light bulbs, by candles, and other light sources. Light travels in straight lines. Light can travel through any substance which is transparent. It travels at different speeds in different substances. It travels fastest through a vacuum, such as through space. Its speed is then 300 000 km per second. *Nothing* can travel faster than this. Telescopes, cameras, and other optical instruments such as camera obscuras, like this one in Edinburgh use the properties of light to form images we can see and interpret.

Shadows

When a light shines on a solid object, a shadow forms behind the object. Light travels in straight lines, so no light from the source can get directly behind the object. A shadow can't have a life of its own! It is simply the area behind the object where the light is missing.

Shadow stick

These students are out in the sunlight. They have put a vertical stick about a metre long in the ground. They are marking the end of the shadow with a stone. In an hour they will come back and mark the new position of the shadow.

Transparent and opaque substances

Opaque materials, like wood or metal, don't let light pass through them. Glass, acetate sheets, and some clear plastic containers are **transparent**, and let light through so no shadow forms behind them. But there are other materials, such as greaseproof paper and frosted glass, which might let some light through. These are called **translucent** materials.

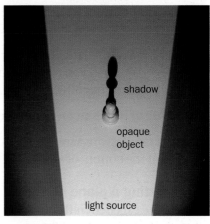

The rays from a torch can't bend round chess pieces. Shadows form behind them. A taller king would have a longer shadow than a short pawn.

1 What is a light source? Give some examples. ▲
2 Write down two facts about light rays. ▲
3 In the drawing of the shadow stick, which way will the shadow move during the day? ▲
4 What does this show about the direction in which the Sun seems to move? ▲

5 What happens to the length of the shadow as the Sun gets lower in the sky?
6 Describe the shadows which you see when light shines on
  a a clear lemonade bottle
  b a translucent plastic milk bottle
  c a drinks can.
7 Explain why the story about Peter Pan's shadow is make-believe.

DID YOU KNOW?

➲ In J M Barrie's story about Peter Pan, Peter's shadow fell off, and Wendy had to sew it back on again!

55

You see a light source when its light travels directly to your eye. But you can see other objects when light is reflected from them.

If you shine a ray of light at a flat (or **plane**) mirror, it is reflected in a definite direction. If you measure the angle of incoming (**incident**) light, and the angle of the **reflected** light, they are always equal to each other.

The angle of incidence = the angle of reflection.

The next two drawings show light from a torch being shone onto different surfaces at the bottom of a dark box.

Light hitting a plane mirror

Mirrors are excellent reflectors because the surface of the mirror is very smooth. If you shine parallel rays of light at it from a torch all the rays of light reflect at the same angle. A great deal of light is reflected in this direction. If your eye is in the right place, it can see this bright beam of light. If your eye is in a different position it doesn't see the beam.

Light hitting a piece of paper

Compared with a mirror, the surface of a piece of paper is dull and rough. Each bit of the surface is at a different angle to the next. Each incoming ray of light obeys the reflection rule. But the rays hit pieces of the surface which are at various angles. The result is that light is reflected from the paper, not in a single beam, but in many different directions. It is scattered. Wherever your eye is, it can see some of this scattered, reflected light. The rougher the surface, the more the light is scattered, and the duller it looks.

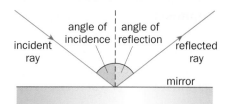

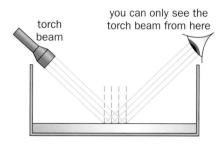

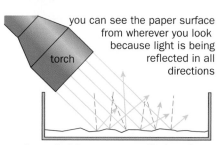

surface of white paper magnified to show roughness

Polished tables and floors makes the surface smoother so it reflects more light and looks brighter.

If you're walking or cycling on dark roads, make sure you can be seen. Wear light coloured clothing or reflector strips to reflect as much light as possible.

Some road signs use material with tiny shiny balls embedded in the surface. This shiny material reflects lots of light in all directions.

1 When light is reflected in a mirror, what is special about the angle of the incident and reflected rays? ▲

2 What can you see in a completely darkened room? ▲

3 If you put a lamp in this dark room as a light source, explain how you could now see
  a the lamp
  b a piece of white paper.

4 How do different types of reflector strip work in order to make cyclists more visible?

5 **Try to find out** how different surfaces appear when you shine a torch on them in a darkened box. How would dust on a mirror affect the way it can reflect light?

When you look into a plane mirror, you can see yourself. Your image appears to be behind the mirror and the same size as you. But when you look into a curved mirror, strange things happen!

There are two types of curved mirror, **convex** and **concave**. (For a con*cave* mirror, the shiny side *caves* in.)

Convex mirrors

If you look into a convex mirror you can see a lot of your surroundings, but the image appears smaller than normal.

If you shine a light into a convex mirror, the rays obey the reflection rule and spread out.

Concave mirrors

If you look at close up things in a concave mirror you see a **magnified** image. If you look at far off things, they appear smaller and upside-down.

If you shine a light into a concave mirror, the rays obey the reflection rule and are brought in to a focus.

Solar furnace

The Sun's rays can be collected by any concave shiny surface to produce heat.

This furnace can produce a temperature of around 3500 °C, enough to melt the metal tungsten.

On a small scale, the Sun's energy can be used for cooking.

DID YOU KNOW?

➲ Concave mirrors several metres in diameter are used in astronomical reflecting telescopes. The large area is able to collect dim light from the stars.

1 What types of mirror could you use for make-up or shaving? What would be the advantage of each type? ▲
2 If a driver has one convex and one plane rear-view mirror, how would the images in each be different? ▲
3 Why could you not use a concave mirror as a rear-view mirror?
4 List as many different uses as you can for each of the three types of mirror.
5 **Try to find out** what happens when you use a concave mirror to focus light from a window onto a sheet of paper.

Lenses come in various shapes. The two common types are **concave** and **convex**. (Remember that a con*cave* surface *caves* in.)

Concave lens

If you look through a concave lens you can see a lot of your surroundings. The image appears smaller than normal, and it is always upright.

Convex lens

A convex lens can behave in different ways, depending on where you hold it.

Held close to an object, you can use it as a magnifying glass. The image is **magnified** and the right way up.

Holding it at arm's length, and looking at a distant object, the image appears smaller than normal, but it is upside down.

How do lenses work?

Light travels in straight lines. But when it passes through the lens, it is bent. Because of this, when you look through the lens, the light appears to be coming from a different direction.

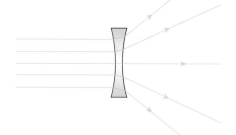

A concave lens spreads the rays of light out.

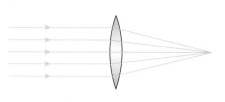

A convex lens focuses the rays of light to a point.

1 a What kind of lens would you use as a magnifying glass? ▲

 b In what way would the thickness of a convex lens affect what you saw? ▲

2 List some things that convex lenses and concave mirrors have in common. ▲

3 Try to find out how lenses are made.

Projecting an image on a screen

If light is shone through a convex lens, it will be bent by the lens and brought to a focus.

These students are projecting an image of the lab window onto a paper screen. They can use different strength lenses, and they can alter the position of the screen and the lens. By carefully adjusting the distance of the lens to the screen, they can produce a sharply focused image. If the distance isn't quite right, the image is blurred.

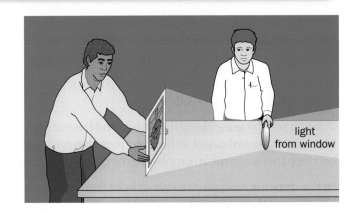

light from window

Lenses doing different jobs

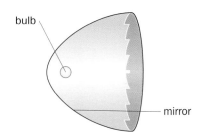

bulb

mirror

In certain cases, the lens of someone's eye may have difficulty in focusing light on the retina at the back of the eyeball. Spectacle lenses are used to correct this fault. They can be concave, convex, or a mixture of the two.

Both the curved reflector at the back of a car headlight, and the glass at the front, help to produce a focused beam. Instead of being a thick convex lens, though, the inside of the lens has a jagged shape.

Camera lenses are often made up of groups of lenses made of different types of glass. This helps to reduce the colour fringes produced by a single lens.

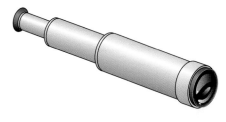

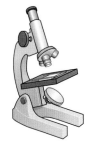

A simple refracting telescope has a thin convex lens at the front, and a smaller fatter convex lens for the eyepiece. This produces an inverted image.

In a microscope, a series of lenses is used to produce a large image of a tiny object. Again, the image is inverted.

In binoculars, or a bird-watching telescope, it is important that the image is upright.

1 List five instruments which use lenses. ▲
2 What shape of lens would be used to correct the sight of a person whose eyeball was longer than normal?
3 Copy the drawing of the Fresnel lens of the car headlight and draw light rays

to show how the light will be bent into a beam. ▲
4 **Try to find out:** A simple telescope gives an inverted image. Try to find out the arrangement of lenses in a telescope which could be used for bird watching.

DID YOU KNOW?

The jagged lens in a car headlight, or in an overhead projector, or in a stage light is called a Fresnel lens. It uses less glass and is lighter than the same strength convex lens.

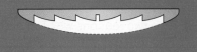

You have seen that lenses seem to be able to alter the behaviour of light. This happens because light bends as it passes from one transparent material to another. This bending is called **refraction**.

When you go to the swimming baths, you will have noticed that the water looks shallower than it really is.

You can see the same thing happen in the laboratory by standing a glass block on a piece of paper. When you look down through the block, a mark on the paper underneath appears to be closer than it really is.

In the drawing, you can see rays of light from the mark on the paper. They go upwards through the block, and then bend at the surface. Your eye sees the rays after they have been bent. The rays of light appear to have come from a point about a third of the way up the block. This is where the mark on the paper *appears* to be.

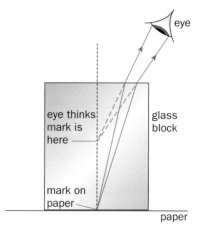

Measuring angles

If you pass a beam of light through a rectangular glass block, the ray of light is refracted as it enters and as it leaves the block, as shown in this photograph.

Tim and Tina decide to investigate how this happens. They decide to shine the incoming light in different directions and to measure the angles of incidence and refraction. This is what they measured.

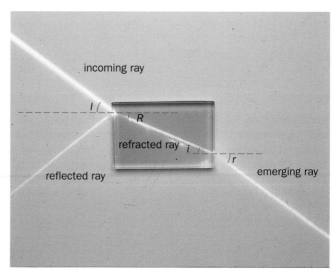

I	R	i	r
15°	10°	10°	15°
30°	19°	19°	30°
45°	28°	28°	45°
60°	35°	35°	60°

They found that the emerging ray is always parallel to the incoming ray.

1 When you look through the front of a fish tank, why do the fish look closer than they really are? A drawing may help.

2 What could Tim and Tina say about the directions of the incoming and emerging rays?

3 What would happen if they shone a ray of light at right angles to the surface of the glass block?

4 Give two reasons why Tim and Tina found that the emerging ray was dimmer than the incoming ray.

5 If they had arranged the incoming ray of light at the bottom of the glass block instead of at the top, do you think they would have got the same measurements? Explain your answer.

6 Make a list of other examples of refraction that you have seen or know about.

DID YOU KNOW?

➲ Refraction occurs because light slows down in denser materials.

➲ The speed of light in a vacuum is about 300 000 km/s (actually 299 793 km/s). In water it is about 225 000 km/s. In different types of glass it is usually between 150 000 and 200 000 km/s.

➲ The speed of light in air, at 299 705 km/s, is only slightly slower than in a vacuum. (But this is still 900 000 times faster than the speed of sound in air!)

When a beam of white light is refracted, something else happens. It is **dispersed** into different colours. You can see **dispersion** if you shine a beam of white light through a **prism** (a triangular piece of glass or plastic).

The continuous spread of colour is called a **spectrum**. This ranges from reddish colours at one end, through the greeny-blues, to the 'purplish' colours indigo and violet. This is the spread of colour you see in a rainbow. Red light is refracted the least. Violet light is reflected the most. Although you can't see them, infra-red and ultra-violet rays could be present, at either end of the visible spectrum.

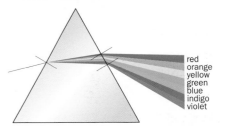

red
orange
yellow
green
blue
indigo
violet

Rainbows
A rainbow forms when sunlight from behind you is refracted, dispersed, and reflected from raindrops in front of you.

Getting back to white
The prism splits light into a spectrum of colours. It looks as though white light consists of a mixture of all these different colours. To check this, you can pass the coloured light through a second prism. The spectrum is recombined to form a single white beam again.

1 Write down the seven colours of the visible spectrum in order, starting with red. What do the initial letters of these colours spell? What do they spell backwards? (Remembering one of these words can help you to remember the order of the spectrum colours!) ▲

2 Does the spectrum *really* consist of seven separate colours? ▲

3 Where else can you find evidence that 'white' light is made up of different colours? ▲

4 If you were facing a rainbow, where would your shadow be? ▲

5 **Try to find out** what would happen if you used a second prism to try to split the coloured light from the first prism into further colours. What would this tell you about the coloured light and white light?

DID YOU KNOW?

➲ If you face the top of the rainbow, the Sun is directly behind you. The angle between your eye, each part of the rainbow, and the Sun is about 42°.

You can protect your eyes from bright light with sunglasses. The lens material cuts out, or **absorbs**, some of the light reaching your eye. Some types of lens have a mirrored surface which also reflects some of the light.

You could design an experiment to test the efficiency of various sunglasses. You might need a ray box to shine a bright beam of light at the lens, and a light meter to measure the amount of light being reflected by, or transmitted through, the material. You would have to think about how to shield out any room lighting.

Mixing coloured lights

We can also mix coloured lights together. For lights, the three **primary** colours are red, blue, and green. Mixing them all together gives white light.

The three **secondary** colours here are cyan, yellow, and magenta.

Red and blue light give magenta. Blue and green light give cyan. Green and red light give yellow.

Red, blue, and green together give white.

Coloured filters

If you shine a beam of light through a coloured filter, some colours are blocked, or **absorbed**. Others are **transmitted** through the filter.

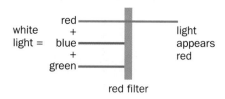

A red filter absorbs blue and green light and transmits red light.

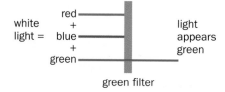

A green filter absorbs red and blue light and transmits green light.

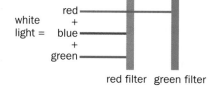

The red filter absorbs blue and green light. The green filter absorbs the red light. No light passes.

1 If you were testing sunglasses with the equipment described at the top of the page,
   a Explain what measurements you would need to make.
   b Describe some of the precautions you would have to take to make your comparisons fair.
   c Say how you would judge which glasses would protect your eyes best. ▲

2 You could do a similar experiment to classify any group of transparent, translucent, and opaque materials.
   a How would you classify an opaque material?
   b How would you decide whether a material was transparent or translucent?

3 a What colours of light will a blue filter absorb?
   b What colour of light will a blue filter transmit?
   c Make a drawing to show this.

4 What will you see when you look at a white light through a red and green filter together?

Mixing coloured pigments

Red, blue, and yellow are the **primary** colours for paints. Red mixed with blue gives magenta. Blue mixed with yellow gives green. Yellow mixed with red gives orange. Magenta, green, and orange are the **secondary** colours for paints.

Shining white lights onto coloured surfaces

White objects reflect white light. Now, you can think of white light as a mixture of red, green, and blue light. So a white object can reflect red, green, and blue light. It can also reflect various mixtures of red, green, and blue light.

If you shine a beam of light onto a coloured surface, some colours are **absorbed**. Others are **reflected** by the surface.

DID YOU KNOW?

➲ Many disco and stage lighting effects depend on shining coloured lights on coloured surfaces.

MANY STAGE LIGHTING EFFECTS DEPEND ON SHINING COLOURED LIGHTS ON COLOURED

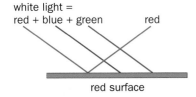

A red surface absorbs blue and green light and reflects red light.

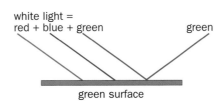

A green surface absorbs red and blue light and reflects green light.

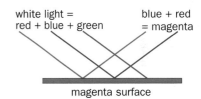

A magenta surface absorbs green light and reflects red and blue light.

The appearance of coloured surfaces in coloured light

Cars can appear unusual colours in street lights.

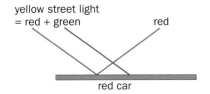

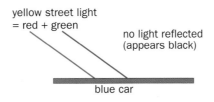

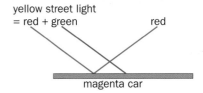

Imagine you were wearing a yellow shirt. At a disco, this would appear to change colour in different light.

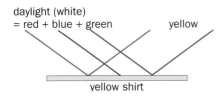

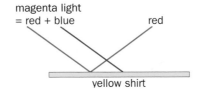

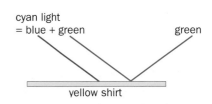

QUESTIONS

1 Draw diagrams to show what colour a yellow surface would appear in:
   a red light   **b** green light
   c blue light   **d** yellow light.
2 Green plants use light energy to grow. What would happen to plants in a dark greenhouse if they were lit only by green light?
3 Why is it important for people who match paints for car repairs, or who match fabric dyes, to work under controlled lighting conditions?
4 Try shining coloured lights on the 'Did you know?' panel. Which words seem to disappear under which lights?

How sounds are made

Sound, like light, is a kind of energy. In a band, different types of instruments make different sounds. But they all have one thing in common. Sounds are made when something vibrates. In a guitar, it's the strings which vibrate. In a drum, the drum-skin vibrates.

In a saxophone, the air inside it vibrates. Even the singer's vocal cords vibrate (you can feel this yourself if you hold your hand to your throat and say 'Aah'!). And when you hear a sound, your eardrum and the bones inside your ear vibrate before sending the message to your brain. You can feel and see these vibrations for yourself:

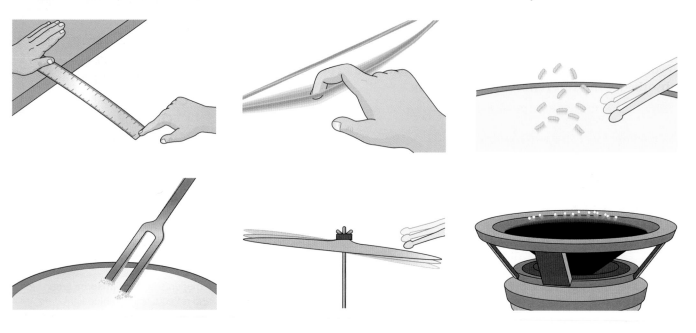

Altering sounds

You can alter a sound in two ways. You can alter its **volume** (make it louder or softer). Or you can alter its **pitch** (make it higher or lower).

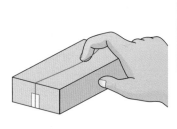
You can make louder notes by plucking the string harder.

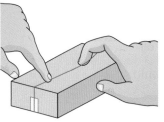
You can make higher notes by tightening the string, or by shortening the vibrating part.

You can make softer notes by blowing more gently.

You can make lower notes by emptying water out to make a longer column of air.

1 How are all sounds made? ▲
2 What makes the sound when you are playing
   a a drum
   b a guitar
   c a saxophone? ▲

3 Make a list of musical instruments
   a which you hit
   b which you blow
   c which have vibrating strings.

DID YOU KNOW?
➲ The pitch of a bongo drum can be changed. When the player squeezes the drum between his knees, the cords tighten the drum-skin and it plays a higher pitched note.

How sound travels – music to your ears

If you're listening to a drummer at a concert, you don't have to put your ear on the drum-skin to hear the beat. Sound can travel through the air. The sound is carried to your ears by vibrating air molecules.

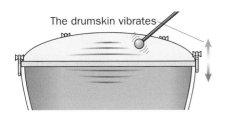

The drumskin vibrates

When the drummer strikes the drum, the drumskin vibrates rapidly up and down.

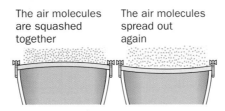

The air molecules are squashed together

The air molecules spread out again

The vibrating drumskin makes the molecules vibrate backwards and forwards. These molecules affect the molecules next to them. The sound spreads out.

The sound spreads out in all directions

Within a fraction of a second, all the air molecules in the theatre will be vibrating. You hear sound when the air inside your ear starts to vibrate.

In fact, sound can travel through all substances, solids, liquids, and gases – anywhere where the sound can be passed on by vibrating particles. And the more tightly packed the particles are, the further the sound travels. Dolphins communicate by sending out high-pitched squeaks and clicks which travel through the water.

Will sound travel through a vacuum?

In this demonstration, an electric bell is hung inside a bell jar. Even though it is inside, you can hear the bell quite clearly.

But when the air is pumped out of the jar, you can't hear the bell at all. Once the air molecules have been removed, there is nothing for the sound to travel through.

When air is let in, you can hear the bell again.

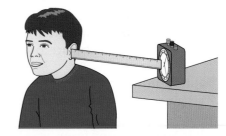

If you hold one end of a ruler to your ear, and the other end to a clockwork timer, you can hear the ticking through the wood.

1 What evidence is there that sound travels through
  a solids
  b liquids
  c gases? ▲
2 Why can't sound travel
  a in a vacuum
  b on the Moon? ▲
3 Draw a bar chart to show the speed of sound in various materials. ▲
4 You can sometimes see a water-mechanic listening to pipes in the road through a long metal rod. Why do they do this? ▲
5 In old-fashioned Wild West films, the hero sometimes puts his ear to the railway track. What advantage does this have? ▲
6 Try to find out:
  a how a ship's echo sounder measures the depth of the water.
  b Why in a thunderstorm you see the flash before you hear the bang.

DID YOU KNOW?

➲ Sound travels at different speeds in different substances. Here are some approximate values:

air	330	metres per second
water	1400	metres per second
brick	3600	metres per second

Too much noise – noise pollution

Noise pollution can be a real problem today. Traffic noise can be a nuisance in houses built close to main roads. The noise of personal stereos and lawnmowers can be a nuisance to old people who want to sleep in their gardens on a sunny afternoon! Even in school, too much noise can be a problem. You can measure noise levels with a sound meter. This has a microphone which converts sound energy levels into electrical energy to display on a scale. Noise levels are measured in **decibels** (dB).

Acceptable noise levels

The decibel scale ranges from 0 dB, the quietest sound you can hear, to around 180 dB, the sound close to a space rocket launch.

As the scale increases by 10 dB, the loudness gets ten times larger. So 40 dB is ten times louder than 30 dB. And 90 dB is 10,000 times louder than 50 dB. A noise above 125 dB can be painful. Long exposure to noise levels above 85 dB can cause permanent damage to your inner ear.

	Examples of decibel levels
0	Quietest sound you can hear
30	Whisper
60	Conversation, dishwasher, washing machine
90	Lawnmower, food processor, lorries, shouting
110	Pneumatic drill, baby crying, car horn, disco
120	Rock concert, clap of thunder
140	Gun blast, aeroplane taking off

Soundproofing

You have seen that sound travels more quickly through solids than through air. And sound can travel much further through hard solids. You can use soft foams, waddings, and fabrics as soundproofing materials to reduce noise pollution. Even layers of newspaper, or egg boxes, will stop the transmission of sound across a surface.

Too little noise – deafness

Some people would be glad if they could hear more noise! Deafness can have a number of causes. In a family where a number of people are deaf, the cause can be due to heredity. Some people's deafness is caused by working in a noisy environment, or listening to loud music for long periods. Other causes are from disease, accidents, or simply due to growing old. Modern hearing aids can be of great help to deaf people. They amplify the sounds that aren't being heard so well. Some deaf people learn to lip-read, as this helps them to understand sounds that they can't hear.

Just as you may wear sunglasses to absorb bright light, it is sometimes necessary to wear ear-protectors to absorb loud noise. In these ways we can protect our eyes and ears from damage.

---

1 A small cardboard box with an electric bell suspended in it by rubber bands is used to test the soundproofing qualities of different materials.
  a How effective would you expect plastic foams, aluminum foil, towelling, newspaper, and egg box card to be?
  b What effect will the thickness of the material have?
2 Design an experiment where you could measure the sound levels of various activities
  a in the classroom
  b around school
  c at home.

DID YOU KNOW?
➡ Normal double glazing doesn't cut out much sound. The air gap has to be more than 10 cm before noise levels are reduced.

Frequency and pitch

The pitch of a sound (how high or low the sound is) depends on how rapidly the 'sound producer' vibrates.

The frequency of a sound is the number of sound vibrations set up in **1 second**. It is measured in hertz (Hz). When you pluck the top string of a guitar, it vibrates 660 times in 1 second. The frequency of the sound it makes is 660 Hz. When you pluck the bottom string, it vibrates only 165 times each second, giving a sound with frequency 165 Hz.

The higher the frequency of a sound, the higher is its pitch.

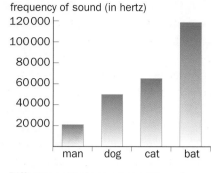

Different animals can hear different frequencies of sound.

Amplitude and volume

The loudness of a sound depends on the **amplitude**, or size, of the vibrations. A large amplitude produces a loud sound, small amplitude produces a soft sound.

You can use a microphone and oscilloscope to show this relationship. When you speak into the microphone, it converts mechanical vibrations in the air into electrical vibrations which can be displayed on the oscilloscope. You can use a signal generator and an oscilloscope to see the relationship between the amplitude and frequency of a vibration, and the sound it makes.

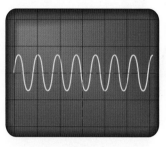
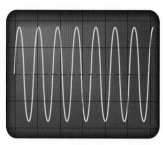

soft   loud

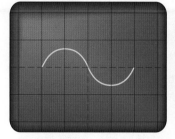
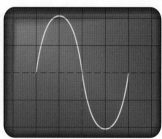
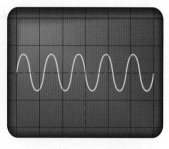
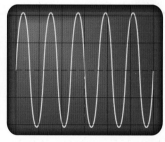

This note has a low pitch and sounds soft. Low frequency, small amplitude.

This note has a low pitch and sounds loud. Low frequency, large amplitude.

This note has a high pitch and sounds soft. High frequency, small amplitude.

This note has a high pitch and sounds loud. High frequency, large amplitude.

QUESTIONS

1 What is meant by:
   a the pitch
   b the frequency of sound? ▲

2 The frequency of a drum note is 20 Hz. What does this tell you about the drum-skin movement when it is struck?

3 Will your vocal cords be vibrating more rapidly when you give a high pitched scream or a low growl?
   Explain your answer. ▲

4 As people get older, they may lose the ability to hear high frequency sounds. Why might this be a problem?

5 Explain the difference in the sounds which a porpoise uses for
   a communication
   b navigation.

6 **Try to find out** why you don't hear a dog whistle properly.

DID YOU KNOW?

➲ Porpoises communicate using low frequency barks, moans, and whistles. They send out large amplitude, high frequency sounds to help them navigate.

➲ Bats also emit high frequency sounds. They avoid obstacles by detecting the echoes from them.

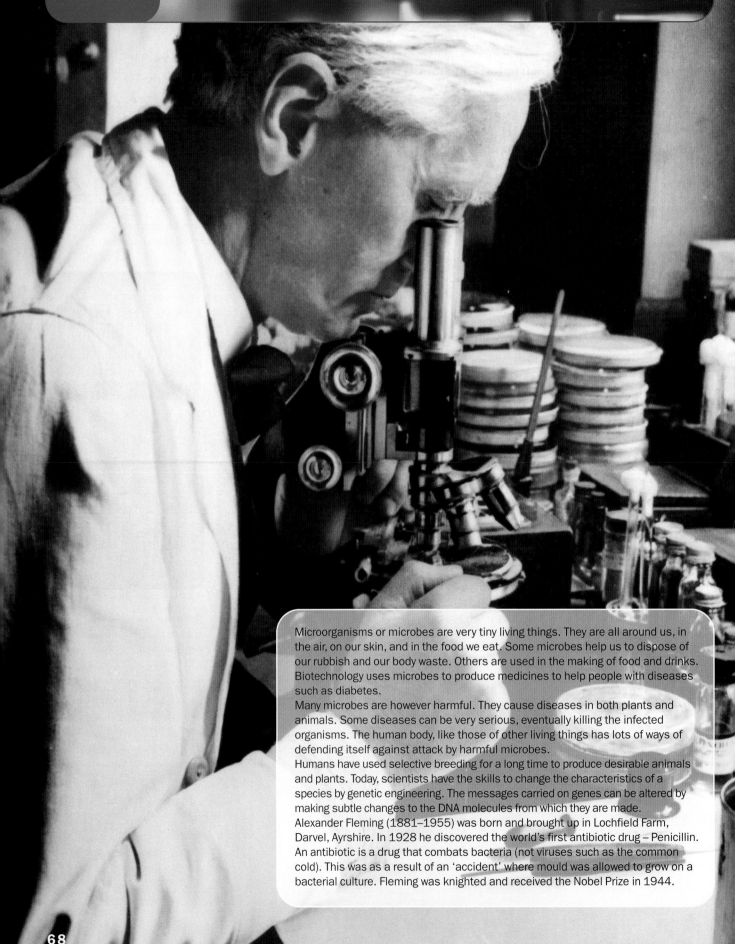

16 Microorganisms /biotechnology

Microorganisms or microbes are very tiny living things. They are all around us, in the air, on our skin, and in the food we eat. Some microbes help us to dispose of our rubbish and our body waste. Others are used in the making of food and drinks. Biotechnology uses microbes to produce medicines to help people with diseases such as diabetes.

Many microbes are however harmful. They cause diseases in both plants and animals. Some diseases can be very serious, eventually killing the infected organisms. The human body, like those of other living things has lots of ways of defending itself against attack by harmful microbes.

Humans have used selective breeding for a long time to produce desirable animals and plants. Today, scientists have the skills to change the characteristics of a species by genetic engineering. The messages carried on genes can be altered by making subtle changes to the DNA molecules from which they are made.

Alexander Fleming (1881–1955) was born and brought up in Lochfield Farm, Darvel, Ayrshire. In 1928 he discovered the world's first antibiotic drug – Penicillin. An antibiotic is a drug that combats bacteria (not viruses such as the common cold). This was as a result of an 'accident' where mould was allowed to grow on a bacterial culture. Fleming was knighted and received the Nobel Prize in 1944.

Microorganisms (or microbes for short) are very tiny living things that can only be seen with a microscope. There are millions and millions of them in the air around us, in the soil, in water, and in our bodies.

The three main types of microbes are bacteria, viruses, and microscopic fungi.

Bacteria

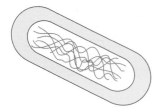   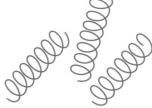

Bacteria are cells with no nucleus.   rod shaped bacteria   round bacteria   spiral shaped bacteria

Bacteria are very small living cells. They are unusual in that they do not have a nucleus. The information needed to control the cell is carried on a single thread of DNA.

Bacteria reproduce by dividing into two. In the right conditions they can reproduce very quickly – about once every 20 minutes.

Viruses

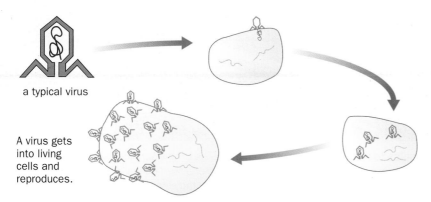

a typical virus

A virus gets into living cells and reproduces.

Viruses are much simpler than bacteria. They are also about 100 times smaller than bacteria so they can't be seen under an ordinary microscope. Viruses are not cells, they are just a protein shell with some DNA inside. They can only reproduce inside other living cells. They take over a cell and make it produce more viruses.

Microscopic fungi: these include yeast and moulds

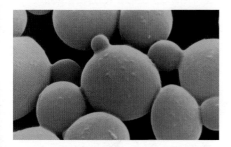   

Yeast cells seen under a microscope are like tiny balls. They reproduce by growing 'buds' on the side. When the buds are big enough they drop off.

Moulds grow in warm, damp places. They are made up of lots of thin threads which grow over and inside their food. Moulds feed on dead things. They reproduce by releasing spores into the air.

1 What are microorganisms? ▲
2 How are bacteria different from other cells? ▲
3 Some people say that viruses are not living things. Give one reason why:
   a they could be right
   b they could be wrong.
4 What is the difference in the way that yeast and moulds reproduce?
5 **Try to find out** how mould fungi release their spores into the air.

Many microbes feed on the remains of dead animals and plants. They produce enzymes which make the dead things rot or **decompose** into a liquid. They then feed on this liquid.

Microbes which make things rot are called **decomposers**. Decomposers are important because they get rid of dead plants and animals and turn them into useful chemicals in the soil.

Decomposers are very useful in sewage works, where they break down human waste, and in compost heaps, where they break down waste plant material. Materials that can be decomposed by microbes are called **biodegradable**.

Sewage works

Sewage consists of urine and faeces from our bodies, water from washing, and some industrial wastes. It also contains some harmful microbes that could spread disease. These things must be removed from the sewage so the water leaving the works is safe.

> ### DID YOU KNOW?
> ⊃ Anything made from plant or animal mattter is biodegradable. This includes paper, wool, cotton, and leather.
> ⊃ Things that won't decompose are called non-biodegradable. Most plastics are non-biodegradable.

Raw sewage is left to settle in large tanks. Faeces settle to the bottom to form sludge. This is later used to make fertilizer and methane gas.

The liquid from the tanks is now sprinkled over stones covered in bacteria. These bacteria feed on any waste that is left in the liquid. Once this is done the clean water is pumped into rivers or the sea.

Making compost

Every year we throw away thousands of tonnes of household and garden waste. Over half of this can be turned into compost.

A compost heap is simply an environment where decomposition is speeded up. To encourage a strong population of decomposer microbes they must have the right conditions. Turning the compost regularly makes sure that all the compost gets enough air and stays at an even temperature.

A good compost bin has ...

... a lid to keep rain out and heat in ...

... air holes to let air get into the heap ...

... an open bottom to allow microorganisms from the soil to get into the heap.

1 a What are decomposers?
  b Why are decomposers useful? ▲
2 How do decomposers get their food? ▲
3 What are biodegradable materials? ▲
4 a What is sewage?
  b Why is it harmful? ▲
5 What things do microbes need to grow in a compost heap?
6 **Try to find out** what happens to 'green waste' in your area.

If our food is left about, it is attacked by microbes which then decompose it. Usually unpleasant or poisonous substances are produced which can make us ill.

However, not all microbes turn food into nasty substances. Sometimes the result can be pleasant to eat.

Cheese and yoghurt are made by microbes (or by the enzymes taken from them).

Cheese

Milk already has microbes in it. These usually make it go sour and lumpy. The lumpy bits are called curds. Curds can be changed into cheese by adding more microbes. Different sorts of microbes make different sorts of cheese. The bubbles in this cheese are made by bacteria as they respire.

Yeast is a microscopic fungus which feeds on sugar. It is able to release energy from sugar **without** oxygen. The process is called **fermentation**.

Yoghurt

Yoghurt is also made by adding bacteria to milk. The milk is usually boiled first to kill off any unwanted microbes. Bacteria are then added and these release enzymes into the milk. These enzymes make the milk go thick and slightly sour. Flavourings are added to yoghurt to change the taste.

There are two waste products from fermentation; carbon dioxide gas and liquid alcohol. Fermentation has been used for hundreds of years for baking and brewing.

Baking

Bakers add yeast to dough to make it rise. Yeast feeds on the sugars in the dough and produces bubbles of carbon dioxide. This makes the dough swell. During baking, the yeast is killed and fermentation stops. The smell associated with baking bread comes from the alcohol as it evaporates away! The holes you see in baked bread are where yeast cells produced carbon dioxide.

Brewing

Wine is made as yeast feeds on the sugars in fruit. Most wine is made from grapes. Different types of grapes produce different wines. Carbon dioxide usually bubbles off as the wine ferments. The sugar in beer making comes from barley seeds. Flavours can be added to give different types of beer. Hops are added to produce the bitter taste in 'bitter beer'.

1 a What are curds?
  b How are curds used to make cheese? ▲
2 Why is milk boiled before it is used to make yoghurt? ▲
3 a What is fermentation?
  b What are the waste products of fermentation? ▲
4 Why are there lots of tiny holes in bread? ▲
5 **Try to find out** what other types of food use microbes in their production.

DID YOU KNOW?
➲ A pot of yoghurt can contain more bacteria than there are people on Earth.

Biotechnology uses microbes to make useful things. It brings together the knowledge of the scientist and the skills of the technologist to provide food, medicines, and new materials for industry. It can also help to clear up much of the waste that pollutes our environment.

Why use microbes?

Microbes grow quickly when given the right temperature and food supply. It is therefore easier to grow microbes in large quantities than to develop ways of growing plant and animal cells on their own. Also, microbes are simple organisms. This makes it easier for scientists to genetically engineer new microbes for specific jobs.

Making human insulin by genetic engineering

Diabetics are unable to produce enough insulin of their own. They used to use insulin from pigs or cattle but because this is not the same as human insulin, it sometimes caused side effects. With genetic engineering, bacteria are used to make human insulin. The idea is that we get a good supply of useful product at a lower cost.

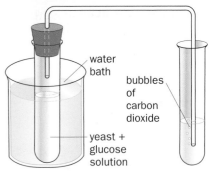

Yeast growing in a laboratory fermenter. If the temperature rises, more carbon dioxide bubbles are produced. More carbon dioxide bubbles means the yeast is fermenting faster.

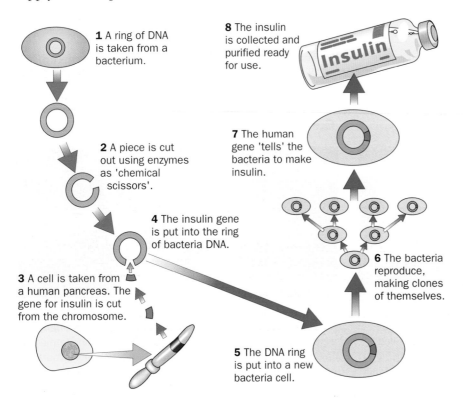

1 A ring of DNA is taken from a bacterium.

2 A piece is cut out using enzymes as 'chemical scissors'.

3 A cell is taken from a human pancreas. The gene for insulin is cut from the chromosome.

4 The insulin gene is put into the ring of bacteria DNA.

5 The DNA ring is put into a new bacteria cell.

6 The bacteria reproduce, making clones of themselves.

7 The human gene 'tells' the bacteria to make insulin.

8 The insulin is collected and purified ready for use.

Insulin

Some diabetics have to inject insulin every day.

DID YOU KNOW?

➲ A mould fungus called *Fusarium* is used to make artificial meat. It has the same amount of protein and fat as meat but a lot more fibre and is cholesterol free. Look out for it on labels at your supermarket – it is called **mycoprotein**.

1 What is biotechnology? ▲
2 Why are microbes used in biotechnology? ▲
3 **a** What is genetic engineering?
  b What is the point of it?
4 Why would a diabetic prefer to use genetically engineered insulin? ▲
5 **Try to find out** what other things are made using genetic engineering.

Diseases can happen when microbes get inside the body. These sorts of diseases are called **infections**.

Most infectious diseases are caused by bacteria and viruses but a few are caused by fungi.

Bacteria
Diarrhoea, whooping cough, pneumonia, tetanus, and blood poisoning are diseases caused by bacteria.

Viruses
Colds, flu, German measles, mumps, chicken pox, small pox, and AIDS are diseases caused by viruses.

Fungi
Athlete's foot and thrush are diseases caused by fungi. The fungi like warm, moist areas such as between your toes or inside the mouth or vagina.

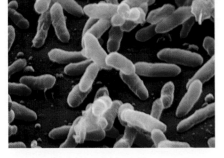
This bacterium causes whooping cough

Measles and chicken-pox are common in childhood

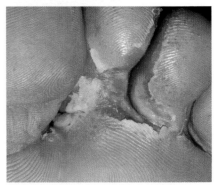
Not deadly, but very uncomfortable

How diseases spread
Diseases can spread in many ways:

- through the breathing system – colds and flu are caused by breathing in viruses from people who cough and sneeze into the air
- through the skin – touching an infected person (or things they have used) can spread viruses that cause chicken pox and measles
- through the digestive system – food and drink can be infected by coughs and sneezes, dirty hands, insects, or unhygienic cooking methods. Food poisoning happens if you eat food and drink infected with bacteria
- through the reproductive system – bacteria that cause sexually transmitted diseases and the virus that causes AIDS pass from one person to another during sexual intercourse.

DID YOU KNOW?
- Viruses can also infect plants.

  This plant has tobacco mosaic virus. Can you think how this disease got its name?

1 What is an infection? ▲
2 Name two diseases caused by
   a bacteria
   b viruses
   c fungi. ▲
3 a What is thrush?
   b Why does it usually only infect the mouth or vagina? ▲
4 Why should you always cough and sneeze into a handkerchief? ▲
5 Give four ways that microbes can get into the body. ▲
6 **Try to find out** what infectious diseases you have had since you were born.

Fighting disease

Your body has lots of ways of defending itself against harmful microbes.

Skin is a very effective barrier against microbes. If the skin gets damaged, the blood quickly clots to repair the hole.

Microbes that do get into the body are attacked by white blood cells. These are the main part of a defence system called the **immune system**. Some white blood cells eat the microbes.

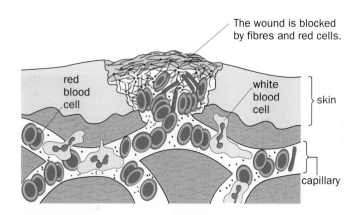

The wound is blocked by fibres and red cells.

red blood cell

white blood cell

skin

capillary

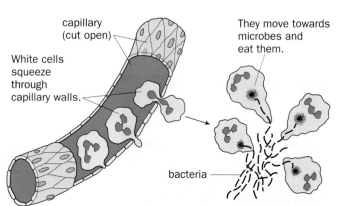

capillary (cut open)

White cells squeeze through capillary walls.

They move towards microbes and eat them.

bacteria

Other white blood cells make chemicals called **antibodies** which kill microbes. Your immune system has a memory. Once you have had a disease you are usually protected from getting it again – you are **immune** to the disease.

Some diseases can make you very ill. You could die before your white blood cells can make enough antibodies to save you. Only **immunization** can protect you.

Dead or weakened microbes are injected into the body. This is called a **vaccine**. They make the body produce antibodies so that the body's defences are ready if the proper disease ever attacks.

How to stop diseases spreading

There are lots of things you can do to avoid catching a disease:

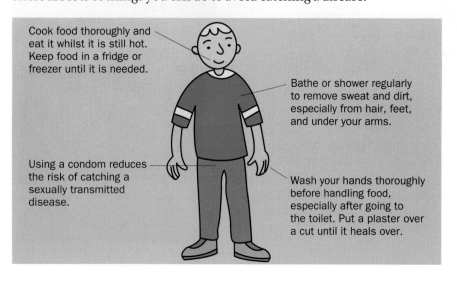

Cook food thoroughly and eat it whilst it is still hot. Keep food in a fridge or freezer until it is needed.

Bathe or shower regularly to remove sweat and dirt, especially from hair, feet, and under your arms.

Using a condom reduces the risk of catching a sexually transmitted disease.

Wash your hands thoroughly before handling food, especially after going to the toilet. Put a plaster over a cut until it heals over.

DID YOU KNOW?

⊃ Antibodies work in different ways. Some make microbes stick together so that white blood cells can eat more of them quickly. Others dissolve the walls of the microbes so that they burst open and die!

1 a Describe what happens if your skin gets damaged.
  b Why does this happen? ▲
2 a What is the immune system?
  b How do you become immune to a disease? ▲
3 a What are antibodies?
  b How do they work? ▲
4 a What is a vaccine?
  b What do vaccines do? ▲
5 Explain why you should bathe or shower regularly. ▲
6 **Try to find out** how many vaccinations you have had and how old you were when you had them.

You have got 46 chromosomes inside the nucleus of every one of your cells. Chromosomes are fine threads that carry 'bits' of information about what you are like. These bits of information are called **genes**. Chromosomes and genes are made of a chemical called **DNA**.

Each of your genes controls one or more of your characteristics that you inherited from your parents. The genes passed on from your father pair up with the genes passed on from your mother. The genes in a pair may carry the same message. But sometimes one of the genes carries a different message from the other. These are called gene **alleles** – different forms of the gene. These alleles are in competition with each other. Some alleles are **dominant** and some are **recessive**. When a dominant allele pairs up with a recessive allele, the dominant allele 'wins' and causes the final effect.

You can show the results of crosses between two people in a genetic diagram. Genes are shown by letters. Capital letters are used for dominant alleles and small letters for recessive alleles. In this diagram H is the allele for black hair and h is the allele for blond hair.

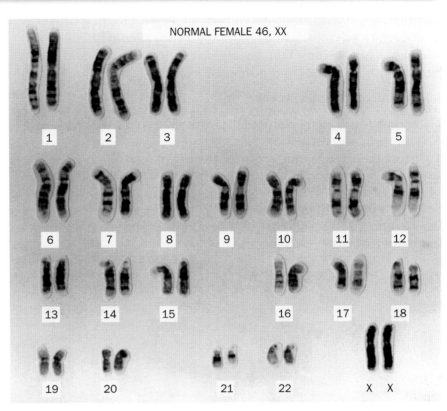

NORMAL FEMALE 46, XX

1 2 3 4 5
6 7 8 9 10 11 12
13 14 15 16 17 18
19 20 21 22 X X

The chromosomes of a human female. They were photographed through a microscope, then cut up and arranged into 23 matching pairs.

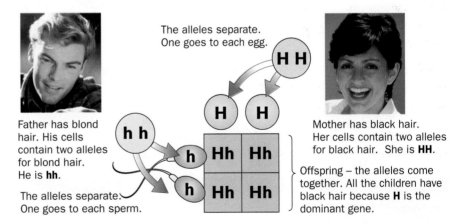

The alleles separate. One goes to each egg.

H H

H H

Father has blond hair. His cells contain two alleles for blond hair. He is **hh**.

h h

h Hh Hh
h Hh Hh

The alleles separate. One goes to each sperm.

Mother has black hair. Her cells contain two alleles for black hair. She is **HH**.

Offspring – the alleles come together. All the children have black hair because **H** is the dominant gene.

1 What are chromosomes and genes made of? ▲
2 A girl inherits one gene allele for blue eyes from her mother and one gene allele for brown eyes from her father. Explain why the girl has brown eyes. ▲
3 What are used to show alleles in a genetic diagram? Give an example. ▲
4 Draw a genetic diagram to show what happens if a woman with Hh alleles has children with a man with Hh alleles. What colour hair will the children have? ▲

DiD YOU KNOW?

◯ Some gene alleles are co-dominant. If two of these get together neither allele wins; instead the final effect is shared. For example a Devon Red bull crossed with a white cow will produce roan (pink) calves.

For thousands of years humans have been selectively breeding farm animals and food crops. Selective breeding is also called **artificial selection**. This is because humans artificially select only the most productive animals and plants to breed from.

Selective breeding works like this:

1 Choose the animals or plants that have the best characteristics.
2 Breed them with each other.
3 Choose the best offspring and breed them with each other.
4 Do this over and over again to improve the characteristics.

Selective breeding in sheep

Sheep are reared for their meat and their wool. A farmer wants big, meaty sheep that have thick, woolly coats.

big meaty male   woolly female

From his flock the farmer selects a big male and a woolly female. These animals are bred together.

The best offspring are chosen and bred together.

The farmer keeps doing this to get a flock of big, woolly sheep.

Selective breeding can be very useful. It has given us...

...beef cattle with more meat...

...dwarf wheat with lots of seeds.

1 Why is selective breeding also called artificial selection? ▲
2 Describe how selective breeding works. ▲
3 A modern cow produces several gallons of milk each day. Explain how farmers have got cows that produce so much milk.

4 Champion male race horses are often 'put to stud'. Racehorse owners pay thousands of pounds to have their female horses mated with the ex-champion. Explain why.
5 **Try to find out** some other examples of selective breeding.

DID YOU KNOW?

➲ All breeds of dogs have been produced by selective breeding. Breeds as different as the Great Dane and the Corgi have descended from the wolf.

Clones are genetically identical organisms. Clones can happen naturally in plants and animals. Today cloning is becoming a high tech business with a lot of plant and animal breeders using the technique.

Natural clones

Many plants, as well as being able to produce seeds, are able to reproduce by growing new parts which can live as separate plants. This is called **asexual reproduction** because no gametes are involved. Some simple animals can also reproduce asexually. The new offspring are exact genetic copies of the 'parent'.

Strawberries send out special stems called **runners** that spread over the ground. New strawberry plants grow at the tips of these stems.

Cloned sheep

In 1997 scientists at the Roslin Institute in Edinburgh cloned a sheep called Dolly. This is how they did it:

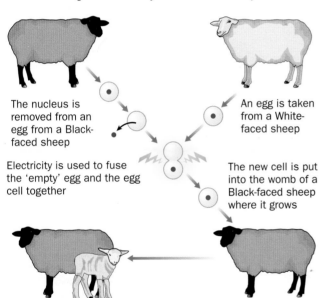

The nucleus is removed from an egg from a Black-faced sheep

An egg is taken from a White-faced sheep

Electricity is used to fuse the 'empty' egg and the egg cell together

The new cell is put into the womb of a Black-faced sheep where it grows

Dolly, a White-faced lamb (clone) is born

Micropropagation

Micropropagation means growing new plants from very small (microscopic) pieces. Some plants can be grown from a tiny piece of plant containing one bud. The pieces are grown in a growth medium containing everything a plant needs for normal healthy growth.

In **tissue culture** new plants are grown from only a few cells (tissue) instead of a bud.

The technique is very quick and doesn't take up much space. Plant growers can use it all year round in a greenhouse to produce healthy disease-free plants.

Seedlings of Douglas Fir trees produced by micropropagation

The problem is...

Cloning reduces the size of the 'gene pool'. There are fewer different genes in the population. Also cloning does not give **genetic variation**. So, if one plant or animal gets a disease it is likely that all the other clones will get it as well. That's why in nature organisms reproduce sexually as well.

DiD YOU KNOW?
➲ Twins are genetically identical – they are clones produced by sexual reproduction.

1 What is a clone? ▲
2 Explain the difference between sexual and asexual reproduction. ▲
3 Give one example of a natural clone produced by
  a sexual
  b asexual reproduction. ▲
4 Give three advantages of tissue culture. ▲
5 Give one big disadvantage of cloning. ▲
6 **Try to find out** more about the arguments for and against cloning.

Chromosomes and genes are made of DNA. DNA stands for **d**eoxyribo**n**ucleic **a**cid. Every chromosome contains one long DNA molecule. The genes are short lengths of DNA. There may be up to 10 000 genes on one chromosome.

DNA is a sort of a plan that determines how the body is made up. Every cell carries a copy of the plan.

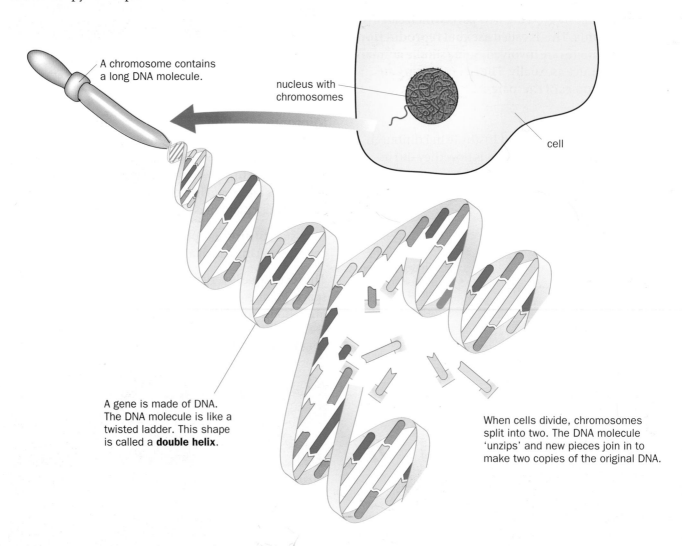

A chromosome contains a long DNA molecule.

nucleus with chromosomes

cell

A gene is made of DNA. The DNA molecule is like a twisted ladder. This shape is called a **double helix**.

When cells divide, chromosomes split into two. The DNA molecule 'unzips' and new pieces join in to make two copies of the original DNA.

Sometime mistakes are made in the copying of DNA. This changes the instructions carried by a gene. This is called a gene **mutation**.

1 What does DNA stand for? ▲
2 Describe the shape of a DNA molecule. ▲
3 a When do DNA molecules make copies of themselves?
  b Describe how DNA molecules make copies of themselves. ▲

4 How might a gene mutation happen? ▲
5 **Try to find out** the names of some genetic diseases caused by gene mutations.

DiD YOU KNOW?
➲ One DNA molecule from the fruit fly, *Drosophila*, is 2.1 cm long!

This is the Fife ethylene plant near Cowdenbeath. It is one of Europe's largest industrial plants used to make ethylene, a chemical needed to make many of our plastics. The plant uses gases from the North Sea which are pumped to it. In it, chemical reactions are used to convert these gases to ethylene. To do this well, the correct temperatures and pressures have to be used and catalysts (chemicals which change the speed of chemical reactions) are needed. It is the engineer's job to work out exactly which conditions produce the ethylene best. All over Scotland, industrial plants like this one make many of the chemicals we need. Some, like a sugar refinery, make substances in crystal form. Some, like an oil refinery, make fuels. But all have to consider carefully how best to produce the chemical, how to make the reactions go at the most appropriate rate, and how to change as much of the starting material into the product as possible. That's the kind of thing this unit is about.

You know it best as a liquid and a solid. It's all round you as a gas. It's essential for life. Water is the most common – and most important – chemical in the world.

Water can change easily from one physical state to another. You can make (solid) ice cubes by **freezing** water in a freezer. In your drink, the (solid) ice **melts** to a liquid again. When you boil a kettle, liquid water **evaporates** to the gas steam. The steam **condenses** to a liquid again when it hits a cold surface (or cold air).

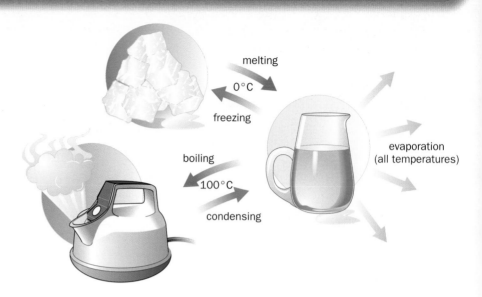

melting
0 °C
freezing

evaporation (all temperatures)

boiling
100 °C
condensing

A closer look at evaporation

When people ask the question *'At what temperature does water change to a gas?'*, the usual answer is '*100 °C*'. But that's not strictly correct: 100 °C is the temperature at which water boils. It's the temperature at which water evaporates fastest.

In fact, liquid water can evaporate to a gas at any temperature between 0 °C and 100 °C. Simple observations will tell you that! The clothes on a washing line will dry without the water boiling. But your observations will also tell you that the clothes will dry quickest on a hot, windy day when they are spread out as far as possible on the washing line. That's because water (like other liquids) evaporates fastest when:

- the temperature is high
- there is air blowing over the water
- the wet material is spread out to give as big a surface area as possible.

1 Ice is one type of 'solid water'. Write down some others.
2 What happens in
  a evaporation
  b condensation? ▲
3 What conditions make water evaporate fastest? ▲
4 We use hair driers and tumble driers to dry things in our homes. How do these two machines help speed up drying?

5 **Try to find out** where in the world will you find
  a large blocks of floating ice
  b jets of hot water coming from the ground
  c masses of ice moving down a mountain? What is each of these called?

DID YOU KNOW?

- 98% of the world's water is in the form of a liquid. Only 2% is ice.
- At altitude, where the air pressure is lower, water's boiling point is also lower. On the top of Ben Nevis, water boils at 96 °C.

Heating molecules makes them move faster and harder. That helps to explain what happens in melting and evaporating.

Water molecules attract each other. In a **lump of solid ice**, the water molecules are held together tightly in rows. They vibrate backwards and forwards.

In a **drop of water**, the molecules move about. They still attract each other but are not held together as tightly as in ice. The drop is a mass of tiny moving molecules. These all have different energies and move about at different speeds.

In **water vapour** (gas), the water molecules are further apart and are not held together. They move around very fast.

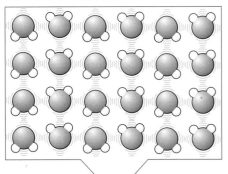

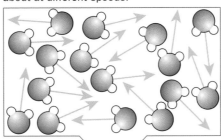

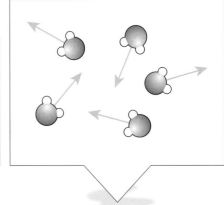

heating to 0°C

ice

water

water vapour gas

When the temperature rises, the extra heat energy makes molecules vibrate faster and harder. At 0°C, the molecules start to break free from the rows and move about. The ice melts.

If a fast-moving molecule is near the surface, it can escape from the other molecules. Of course, you can't see it go. But if the drop is heated, the heat energy gives millions and millions of molecules enough energy to escape. The drop of liquid slowly evaporates.

Cooling has the opposite effect. When heat energy is taken away, the molecules slow down. Then the attraction they have for each other has a bigger effect. When water vapour molecules are cooled, they slow down. When they come into contact they attract each other more. If they are cooled far enough, the attraction will be strong enough to hold the molecules together as liquid water. If they are cooled more, the attractions make the molecules line up into rows to form ice. In ice, the molecules are further apart than they are in water, and so ice is less dense than water

Snowflake – formed in the atmosphere

QUESTIONS

1 What does heating do to molecules? ▲
2 What happens to the water molecules when
   a ice melts
   b water boils
   c water freezes?
   Why does this happen? ▲
3 Snow melts when the temperature rises, but it always seems to be cold when there is a thaw. Why is this?
4 **a** Why does ice float on water? ▲
   b How would the world be different if it didn't?
5 **Try to find out** if there is a temperature at which molecules stop moving.

DID YOU KNOW?

➲ During a thaw, the energy to melt the snow comes from the surroundings, which get colder.

➲ Snowflakes usually form round tiny particles of dust which 'collect' water molecules that freeze on them.

Cloud formation

Clouds can be formed in different ways but two factors are very important. These are:

- **how saturated the air is** (how much water vapour air contains)
  Saturated air is air that can hold no more water vapour. Hot saturated air can hold more water vapour than cold and so, if hot saturated air is cooled, some water has to condense as tiny drops.

- **adiabatic cooling** When the pressure on a gas is reduced and the gas is allowed to expand, it cools down. As the altitude increases, the pressure gets lower. And so, when air is blown over a mountain range, it expands and cools as it rises.

Knowing this, and about freezing, melting, evaporation, and condensing, you should be able to understand the water cycle.

4. As the air rises, the water vapour condenses to form droplets of water. The droplets maybe so small that they are still carried up by the wind, but they gradually grow into bigger drops or freeze into ice crystals. When the air can hold no more, they fall to Earth as rain, sleet or snow.

2. The water vapour is invisible. On a sunny day, all you see is the blue sky! But as the moist air rises, it cools and becomes closer to being saturated.

3. If the wind blows air up over a high mountain, there is a good chance that air will cool so much that some of the water will have to condense. Tiny droplets of water form on tiny particles – dust, volcanic emissions.

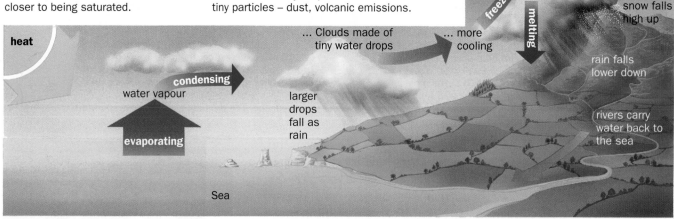

1. Water is continually evaporating from the sea. This happens fastest when wind (especially hot wind) is blowing over the sea.

6. The sea is the world's great reservoir. It 'collects' the run-off water from the land – then it loses it again as it evaporates and the cycle keeps going.

5. Much of the water which falls on the Earth's surface seeps into the ground. (That's where underground springs come from.) Some of it flows into streams and rivers, and then to the rivers and lochs and, eventually, into the sea.

1 What is saturated air? When does saturated air form raindrops? ▲
2 When does adiabatic cooling take place? Why does air cool when it is blown over mountains? ▲
3 Where in the water cycle are there
  a molecules moving about in a liquid
  b molecules fixed in rows
  c molecules breaking free from a solid?
4 Why is the biggest rainfall in Britain found on the country's west side? ▲
5 Sometimes springs seem to appear from nowhere. Where does the water come from? ▲
6 **Try to find out** Britain's wettest spot; the annual rainfall in your town.

DID YOU KNOW?

- Most of Scotland's west coast is hilly. When a south-west wind (the most common wind) blows, moist air is blown up and over the hills. This forms rain which falls on the west side of the country, making it the wettest part.

When you put a crystal of sugar into water, it dissolves. The water separates the sugar molecules which were joined up in the crystal.

The sugar molecules spread through the water.

Because it dissolves, sugar is described as **soluble**. Together, sugar and water make a **solution**.

A solution is made whenever two substances mix completely through each other. The substance which dissolves is called the **solute**. The substance which does the dissolving is called the **solvent**. (In this solution, the sugar is the solute. Water is the solvent.)

The same thing does not happen, however, when you put sand in water. The sand does not dissolve. It is said to be **insoluble**.

Soluble and insoluble substances both have their uses. You use a soluble substance whenever you want to spread a substance through water – like salt through soup, sweeteners through fizzy drinks, detergent to wash dishes. But brick, concrete, glass, wood, and paint are all used for house building because they are insoluble and don't dissolve in the rain.

Water can be used to separate soluble from insoluble substances. Much of the world's salt, for example, comes from underground rock salt. In rock salt, the salt is mixed with sand and rock. Pumping down water is one way to get the salt. The salt dissolves but the sand and rock don't. The salt solution is pumped to the surface and evaporated.

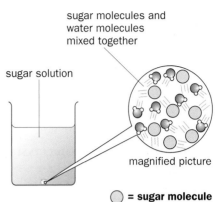

moving water molecules

water (solvent)

molecules in grain of sugar

sugar solution

sugar molecules and water molecules mixed together

magnified picture

grain of sugar (solute)

magnified picture

○ = sugar molecule
🝢 = water molecule

DiD YOU KNOW?
➲ The Romans used to pay their soldiers with salt. That's where the word 'salary' comes from.
➲ Rock salt is used on roads in winter. The sand helps the grip. The salt helps the ice melt.

QUESTIONS

1 What is
  a a solute
  b a solvent
  c an insoluble substance? ▲
2 Name
  a the solvent
  b one solute in the sea.
3 Why is it important to use insoluble substances for building? ▲
4 a How can pure salt can be obtained from underground rock salt?
  b Design an experiment to get salt from rock salt in the lab. ▲
5 Salt is obtained by evaporating sea water in big outdoor 'salt pans' in Saudi Arabia. Explain why this method is not used in Britain.
6 **Try to find out** the solutes in cola (try looking at a big bottle!)

Rock salt in underground caverns

Salt pan in Saudi Arabia

Copper sulphate dissolves well in cold water. You can dissolve around 24 g of it in 100 cm³ water at room temperature (25 °C) before no more will dissolve.

But if you use 100 cm³ hot water,

- 24 g will dissolve quicker
- More copper sulphate will dissolve (around 60 g if the temperature of the water is raised to 60 °C)

Copper sulphate, and other crystals, dissolve better in hot water than in cold.

Saturated solutions

A solution which can dissolve no more solid is called a **saturated solution**. The diagram shows how the amounts of solid dissolved in 100 cm³ saturated solution depend on the temperature of the water.

You can see that for salt, sugar, and potassium nitrate fertiliser (and other solids) hot water dissolves more solid than cold water. For gases, the opposite can be true. Less gas can dissolve in warm water. The bubbles which appear when you warm up water are bubbles of oxygen which can't stay dissolved when the temperature rises.

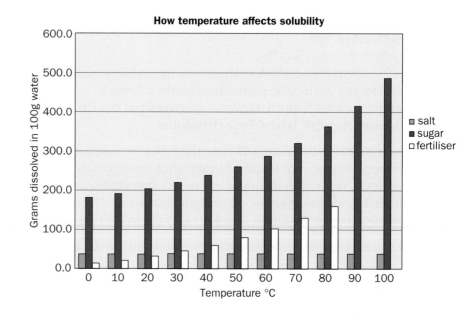

How temperature affects solubility

Grams dissolved in 100g water — Temperature °C

salt ▪ sugar ▫ fertiliser

---

1 How much sugar dissolves in 100 cm³ water
 a at 20 °C
 b at 60 °C? ▲

2 Give two ways in which heating water affects solids dissolving. ▲

3 What is a saturated solution? How would you make one? ▲

4 Does the temperature of the water have a bigger effect on the dissolving of sugar or salt? Explain your answer.

5 Many factories use river water to cool their machines. Hot water is pumped back into the river. How does this affect the river life?

6 Adults often use sweeners instead of sugar in tea and coffee. They have to dissolve quickly. Design an investigation to find out which of 3 powdered sweeteners dissolves best.

7 **Try to find out** the name for the gas which forms bubbles inside a bottle of cola when the Sun shines on it.

DiD YOU KNOW?

- Warm waste water from power stations and factories affect the life in the river. The hot water has less dissolved oxygen for fish and other animals to breathe.

What happens to copper sulphate solutions?

A hot saturated solution (at 60 °C) has 60 g dissolved in it. If this solution is allowed to cool down to room temperature, however, only 24 g copper sulphate can stay dissolved. The rest forms crystals. The slower the cooling, the bigger the crystals.

Growing crystals is called **crystallisation**. Crystallisation can be carried out by allowing hot saturated solutions to cool down. It can also be carried out at room temperature by allowing the solution to evaporate until there is too little water to keep the solid dissolved.

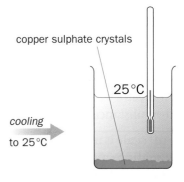

60g more copper sulphate will dissolve

60 °C

heating to 60 °C

Hot saturated solution
At 60 °C, **60 g** of copper sulphate will dissolve.

copper sulphate crystals

25 °C

cooling to 25 °C

Cold saturated solution
Cooling to 25 °C, **24 g** stay dissolved. **36 g** form crystals.

Crystallisation is a very important process. It is used to purify substances. Each time a substance is crystallised, it becomes more pure.

Sugar…

To get sugar from sugar cane, the cane is crushed then sprayed with water to dissolve out the sugar. It is very impure at this stage. In a refinery the sugar solution is treated to remove unwanted substances. Then the water is slowly evaporated to grow crystals. They are not *completely* pure but are pure enough to eat.

Using fungi…

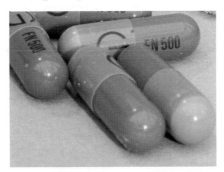

Some important drugs are produced by living things. Penicillin (an antibiotic) is one of these. It is grown by a special fungus. The fungus is treated in different ways to dissolve the drug out of it. After this, the penicillin has to be crystallised several times. That's because it has to be very pure to be used as a medicine.

Diabetes and insulin…

These are crystals of insulin, used to treat diabetes. Scientists wanted to manufacture insulin so they needed to find out exactly what the insulin molecule was like. For that, they needed perfect crystals which could only be grown on a space mission. In space, there is no gravity and not even a tiny movement of the solution to affect crystallisation.

---

1 Describe two ways in which crystals can be grown. ▲

2 How would you grow big crystals of copper sulphate? ▲

3 In winter, puddles of water often have white crystals around them when they dry up. What is this? How was it formed? ▲

4 What is crystallisation? Why is it important? ▲

5 a Why is penicillin crystallised more often than sugar? ▲

b Why have scientists crystallised insulin in space? ▲

6 Try to find out:

a what penicillin is used for

b what diabetes is.

c how insulin used to be produced

Scientists put chemicals which behave in the same way into sets. **Acids** and **alkalis** are two of these sets.

You can find out if a substance is an acid or an alkali by dissolving it and adding universal indicator. The indicator's colour tells what kind of substance you have.

The pH scale is used to measure how acidic or alkaline a substance is. Most of the substances which you handle in the lab have pH values between 1 and 14. A substance with pH 1 is very acidic. A substance with pH 14 is very alkaline. A substance with pH 7 is **neutral** (neither acid or alkali).

Acids and alkalis react with each other. When they are mixed, they **neutralise** each other (cancel each other out).

The experiment on the right shows what happens when acid is added to alkali with universal indicator in it. At the beginning, before any acid has been added, the indicator is violet. Each time acid is added it cancels out some of the alkali. This makes the indicator colour gradually change. Eventually the indicator goes green. Then the solution is **neutral**. Exactly the right amount of acid has been added to cancel out or neutralise all the alkali.

How to find out if a substance is an acid or an alkali

1 Put some water into a test tube

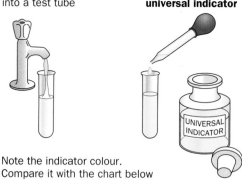

2 Add a few drops of **universal indicator**

3 Add the substance and Shake until it dissolves

4 Note the indicator colour. Compare it with the chart below

Universal indicator colour chart

Very acidic substances	Slightly acidic substances	Neutral substances	Slightly alkaline substances	Very alkaline substances
hydrochloric and sulphuric acid	vinegar fruit juice lemonade	water, sugar and salt	ammonia solution, detergent, baking soda, indigestion mixture	sodium hydroxide (caustic soda)

Neutralising alkali with acid

Acid is added from a syringe

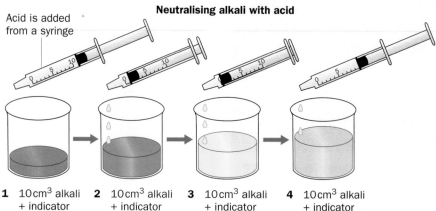

1 10 cm³ alkali + indicator No acid added

2 10 cm³ alkali + indicator + 9 cm³ acid

3 10 cm³ alkali + indicator + 10 cm³ acid added

4 10 cm³ alkali + indicator + 11 cm³ acid added

1 What is
  a universal indicator
  b the pH scale used for? ▲
2 **a** How would you find out if soluble aspirin is acid or alkali?
  b Aspirin solution turns indicator pink. What does this show?

3 What is meant by a neutral substance ? ▲
4 **a** Why do the indicator colour and the pH change in the 'mixing' experiment?
  b Explain the colours and the pH values at **1, 2, 3,** and **4**.
5 **Try to find out** what the word 'acid' means.

DID YOU KNOW?

⊃ Milk's pH changes as it goes sour. Bacteria in the milk produce lactic acid, and the pH goes down from 7 to 4 in around 2 days.

A neutralisation reaction is a reaction in which an acid, or an alkali, is cancelled out.

Neutralisation can be useful

Sometimes, your stomach makes too much acid. This can cause you to suffer from indigestion. Indigestion tablets help to cure the pain. They contain chemicals which cancel out the acid.

Acid rain and acid fertilisers can make the pH of fields too low to grow crops well. To solve this problem, farmers can add lime (an alkali) to neutralise the acid.

Tooth decay is caused by acids made in the mouth. Toothpastes contain chemicals that neutralise the acids and help stop tooth decay. That is why it is important to brush your teeth regularly.

Neutralisation produces salts.

When an alkali is exactly neutralised by an acid, a compound called a **salt** is made. You can't see anything happen when you mix the acid and alkali. (The acid and alkali are colourless solutions. The salt is colourless too.) But when you evaporate off the water, the solid salt is left.

The most commonly made salt in the science lab is **sodium chloride**. It is made by mixing **sodium** hydroxide and hydro**chloric** acid. But there are many other salts, made by mixing different acids and alkalis. Some of these salts are useful as fertilisers, weedkillers, and drugs.

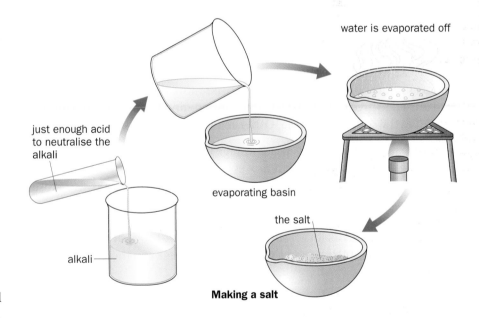

just enough acid to neutralise the alkali

alkali

water is evaporated off

evaporating basin

the salt

Making a salt

1 What is a neutralisation reaction? ▲

2 Why can you use
  a vinegar to treat a wasp sting
  b ammonia to treat a bee sting? ▲

3 a Is baking soda solution acid or alkali (see page 86)?
  b Could you use baking soda solution to treat indigestion

and a nettle sting? Explain your answer.

4 How would you make
  a a salt
  b sodium chloride?

5 Try to find out:
  a which salts are in bath salts and toothpaste
  b why shampoo manufacturers think that pH is important.

DID YOU KNOW?

➲ When you are stung by a nettle, hairs on the nettle leaf inject acid into your skin.

➲ Some types of ant defend themselves by squirting acid at their enemies. Up to $1/5$ of the ant's body weight is made up of acid.

17.3 Colours and flavours

For the enthusiast

Plant indicators

Many of the chemicals which give flowers, leaves, and berries their colours are affected by acid and alkali. The first indicator ever used was litmus, a dye extracted from lichens. It goes red in acid and blue in alkali.

In the diagram, you can see dyes from coloured plants and the colours they go at different pH values. Use the diagrams to answer the questions.

ph	1		7		13
red cabbage		red		green	
red onion		pale red		green	
red grape juice		red	violet	blue	blue-green
beetroot juice	deep red		red	violet	yellow

QUESTIONS

1 Name a plant dye (or dyes) which is
  a violet in water
  b red in acid solution
  c blue in slightly alkaline solution
  d yellow in alkali. ▲
2 Adding
  a sodium hydroxide to red cabbage in vinegar
  b washing soda to red grape juice gives colour changes. What are they?
3 Do you think that universal indicator could have litmus in it? Explain your answer.

DID YOU KNOW?

➲ The colours of some flowers depend on whether they are grown on acid or alkali soil. Can you find out about them?

Acid drinks

Soft drinks wouldn't be the same without acid in them. They are important for the taste and make the drinks more thirst-quenching. Citric acid is used to give the sharp taste in lemonade and fruit juice. Phosphoric acid gives the sour taste in cola. Other acids help the drinks to keep longer.

Unfortunately, there is a big disadvantage in having acid in drinks. For one thing, the acid affects teeth. It removes calcium from them and makes them wear away. But acid is not the only culprit. Sugar in drinks also causes dental decay. Bacteria in the mouth convert the sugar in the drinks into acid in the mouth and the acid then acts on the teeth. Studies have shown that people who drink lots of soft drinks have more tooth decay. A study of English school pupils showed that even 1 can a week can increase tooth decay by 3%!

pH of some common drinks	
Coca Cola	2.4
Diet Coke	3.4
Sprite	2.8
Ribena	3.1
Pepsi	2.5
Orange juice	3.6
Irn Bru	3.3
Lemonade	2-3
Dr Pepper	2.9
Diet Dr Pepper	3.4
Ribena Toothkind	3.9

QUESTIONS

1 Give two reasons why some soft drinks have acid in them. ▲
2 a Give two ways in which soft drinks wear away teeth.
  b *Diet* drinks are better for teeth because they have no sugar in them. Are they better from the *acid point of view*? Explain. ▲
3 Which of the drinks in the table is
  a most acidic
  b least acidic? ▲
4 Is *Irn Bru* more or less acidic than *Sprite*? Explain your answer.
5 Design an experiment to find out how quickly a tooth is eaten away by a soft drink. What would you measure?
6 **Try to find out** why *Ribena Toothkind* is the dentist's friend.

DID YOU KNOW?

➲ Many of the drinks have caffeine in them. That's the same drug as there is in coffee, tea, and chocolate.

➲ Drinking too many soft drinks can affect your weight. One can of non-diet drink has enough sugar (energy) to last you a whole day.

Some reactions are lightning-fast! An explosion, for example, is a reaction which takes place in a fraction of a second. On the other hand, geological reactions take place very slowly. It can take thousands of years to change one type of rock to another.

For reactions like these, it's not possible to do much to make a noticeable change to the reaction's rate. Most reactions, however, take place at a rate which can be speeded up (or slowed down). **The rate of a reaction can be speeded up by:**

breaking down any solids into small pieces:
marble in hydrochloric acid – powdered marble was put in the left hand beaker and lumps in the right hand one.

using more concentrated solutions:
magnesium ribbon in sulphuric acid – more concentrated acid has been used in the right hand test tube.

heating up the materials:
copper will react with oxygen to make black copper oxide, but at room temperature, that takes a very long time. Heating the copper makes the reaction go much faster.

using a catalyst:
(A catalyst is a chemical which changes the speed of a chemical reaction without being changed in the reaction.) If you add a catalyst to a reaction, you can get it back again once the reaction is finished. Hydrogen peroxide reacts to give off oxygen very slowly. When manganese dioxide catalyst is added to the peroxide, oxygen is given off very rapidly. At the end, when the manganese dioxide is filtered off and dried, its mass is the same as it was at the beginning.

DiD YOU KNOW?

➲ Breaking down the marble gives it a bigger surface overall. This means that more of the marble can react because more of it is in contact with the acid.

➲ Flour does not burn well, but fine flour dust can burn explosively if it is spread through the air.

1 Give 4 ways to speed up a chemical reaction. ▲
2 Look at the photographs. Describe what difference it has made:
  a using powdered marble instead of lump
  b using more concentrated acid
  c heating the copper
  d adding manganese dioxide to hydrogen peroxide.
3 What is a catalyst? Explain why manganese dioxide is called a catalyst in the hydrogen peroxide reaction. ▲
4 Why do flour mills have to use huge extractor fans to remove flour dust when flour is being milled?
5 **Try to find out** a reaction which is speeded up by light.

Please don't think that changing reaction rates is only about doing experiments in the science lab. You change reaction rates far more often than you might imagine!

- **You speed up reactions by heating.** That happens in cooking.
- **You slow down reactions by cooling.** You keep food fresh by keeping it cool in a fridge. That slows down the reactions which make it go bad.
- **You speed up reactions by increasing the concentration.** If a fire won't burn, you increase the concentration of oxygen by blowing air over it. If there isn't enough detergent to remove the grease from dishes, you add more and increase the concentration.
- **You speed up reactions by breaking materials into smaller pieces.** If you want to dissolve a jelly, you break it into smaller pieces to speed things up. Small lumps of coal burn more quickly than large ones.

But perhaps you don't think that you use catalysts. You'd be surprised!

If you have a gas powered cordless hair styler, it will have a catalyst inside it. The heat comes from butane gas, but the gas can't burn! Instead, a metal catalyst inside the heater helps the gas to join up with oxygen in the air and give off heat without any flames.

Biological catalysts are called enzymes. 'Biological' washing powders have enzymes in them. The enzymes help the water to break up materials like egg, fat, and perspiration. The wash can be done at a lower temperature, saving energy.

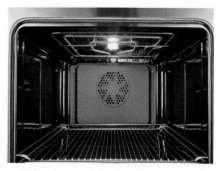

Self-cleaning ovens have walls lined with metal oxide catalyst. When fatty food is being cooked, the fat can 'spark' all over the cooker. Normally the fat would not burn off at the oven temperature but as it lands on the walls, the catalyst helps it join up with oxygen and form a gas.

Most catalysts are used, however, in industry. When a catalyst is used in a reaction, that reaction will go at a good rate at a lower temperature. This means that less heat energy is needed and this cuts down the costs considerably.

QUESTIONS

1 Why are fridges and freezers able to keep food? Which keeps food longest and why? ▲

2 You might use small pieces of coal to start off a coal fire or big lumps if you wanted the fire to burn for a long time. Why? ▲

3 Lighters and some hair stylers use butane fuel but they use the fuel differently. What is the difference? Why is it important? ▲

4 Fat is a compound containing hydrogen and carbon. What is formed when fat joins with oxygen? How does this clean the oven?

5 **Try to find out** some catalysts used in industry.

DID YOU KNOW?

- The margarine you eat is made by reacting vegetable oil with hydrogen – using powdered nickel as a catalyst.
- Denim used to be washed with small pebbles to give it the 'stone-washed' look, but that damaged the fabric. Now enzymes are used instead.

The burning of petrol is one of the most important reactions in use today. The energy it produces is used to power most of our cars and the gases it produces cause major pollution! It's important to keep the level of pollution as low as possible.

Petrol which burns completely does not produce *harmful* substances. Petrol is a mixture of hydrocarbons, (compounds of hydrogen and carbon). The hydrogen joins with the oxygen to make water. The carbon forms carbon dioxide. But, unfortunately, a car engine does not burn petrol completely. The exhaust gases which leave the engine contain unburned hydrocarbon, carbon monoxide, and nitrogen oxides (formed when the electrical spark passes through the air). Small traces of sulphur are also present. All of these pollutants have to be removed.

The job of the exhaust's catalytic converter is to help convert these harmful gases into harmless ones before they escape into the air. The catalyst does this well – but not until the gases which reach it are hot. Most pollution is produced by a car when the engine is cold because the gases react too slowly. Car designers try to get over this by moving the converter close to the engine so that the gases are hotter when they meet the catalyst.

Can you find out the differences between these vehicle fuels?

A catalytic converter is located in the exhaust pipe between the engine and the rear tail pipe. Its job is to remove harmful gases from the engine exhaust 'smoke' and release cleaner gases into the atmosphere.

DID YOU KNOW?

➲ To speed up the reaction between the petrol and the air, the petrol is sprayed into the engine cylinders as fine droplets.

➲ Most of the polluting gases are produced by cars in the first few minutes of their journeys.

QUESTIONS

1 a Which substances are introduced into a car engine cylinder? ▲
  b What makes them join together? What happens next? ▲
2 Why is it an advantage to spray petrol into the engine in drops? ▲
3 Which substances are produced
  a when a car engine is working well
  b when it is not burning the petrol completely? ▲
4 a Which types of pollution are produced by a car engine?
  b What does the catalytic converter do to reduce the pollution? ▲
5 Suggest why most pollution is produced by a car at the beginning of a journey. What have car designers done to improve on this?

Dry ice doesn't last very long at room temperature. Dry ice is *solid* carbon dioxide. It changes directly to a gas at –78.5 °C. If the temperature rises above that, any solid quickly changes to a gas and escapes. The solid dry ice 'disappears'.

When a candle burns, the wax disappears, but this time the process is different. The wax disappears because, when it burns, it joins up with oxygen from the air. This forms carbon dioxide and water vapour, which escape.

dry ice escaping: physical change

We say that the first process is a physical change. **In a physical change, a substance changes its form but is not changed into a new chemical.** The dry ice is made of solid carbon dioxide and the gas which escapes is also carbon dioxide. It would be difficult to do, but it would be possible to change the gas back to solid carbon dioxide again.

The second process is a chemical change. **In a chemical change, a chemical reaction takes place and one (or more) new substances is formed.** When the candle burns, the reaction is:

hydrocarbon (in wax) + oxygen → carbon dioxide + water (vapour)

If you are trying to decide whether a change is a physical change or a chemical one, the question to ask is *'Are new chemicals formed when the change takes place?'*

Try to decide for yourself what kind of change is taking place in each of the processes shown here. Then say why you made your choice.

wax burns to form carbon dioxide and water: chemical change

boiling water

burning toast

electric light

dissolving sugar

lighting a match

frying an egg

rusting steel

The story on this introduction page concerns the naming of electric charges, the force between those charges, and the connection to electromagnetism. It concerns an American and a Scot.

The American was Benjamin Franklin. Among his many discoveries was that lightning was a discharge of electricity. In the early 1750s he had carried out the potentially dangerous experiment of flying a kite in a thunderstorm. He saw that loose fibres on the kite string separated from each other. And he was able to produce sparks between a key tied to the kite string and his finger.

He also studied the 'static' electricity formed when he rubbed various substances with fur or a dry cloth. Franklin knew of two types of electric charge. Rubbing glass produced one type of charge. Rubbing sulphur or resinous materials such as amber produced another type. Charges of the same type repelled each other (like the charges on the kite string above). Charges of different types attracted each other. He decided to call these two types of charge 'positive' and 'negative'. We don't know how he decided that glass would give the positive charge. Perhaps he tossed a coin! But he could equally well have chosen glass to be the negative charge. It would have been easier had he done so!

Later, when electric cells were invented, scientists naturally assigned the direction of the flow of current to be from (+) to (−). A century after that, in 1895, electrons were discovered by J J Thomson. It was only then that it was realized that the electrons were the ones that carried the current, and that they moved in the opposite direction to the *conventional* current idea (as accepted by everyone at the time). However, it was much too late to change Franklin's naming convention. The old naming system works fine for most applications, including electronics.

But you need to remember that electricity is really a flow of negatively charged electrons flowing from negative to positive!

The Scot was John Robison. He was born in Boghall, Stirlingshire, in 1739. He was educated at the grammar school in Glasgow and at Glasgow University. When he was 20 he entered the navy and accompanied Major-General James Wolfe's army to Quebec.

He returned to a lecturing post at Glasgow University, then spent some time in Russia, before returning to Scotland in 1773 to become to become Professor of Natural Philosophy at Edinburgh University. He was one of the leading scientists of the day as well as being an accomplished musician and linguist. Edinburgh still holds records of his lecture notes! In 1769 he showed experimentally that the force between charged bodies varied with the distance between them. Although he got slightly different results for attraction and repulsion, he concluded that doubling the distance reduced the force to a quarter and tripling the distance reduced the force to one ninth. This pattern is called an *inverse-square law*. He made the mistake of NOT publishing his results. Thirteen years later, in 1785, the French scientist Charles Augustin Coulomb confirmed the connection between charge and distance, and so this inverse-square law became known as Coulomb's Law. Electromagnetism also follows this inverse-square connection.

Other things Robison is famous for include making the suggestion to James Watt in 1759 that the steam engine could be used to produce motion (of wheeled carriages); and for being the Board of Longitude's representative in charge of John Harrison's 'chronometer' (for determining longitude) on its test voyage to Jamaica in 1762.

Around the beginning of the 1800s, there was lots of interest in electricity. The first battery had just been invented. Electricity from batteries was used to carry out all sorts of experiments.

In 1820, a Danish scientist called Hans Christian Oersted was giving a lecture in Copenhagen. In it, he carried out an experiment to show (he thought) that there was no connection between electricity and magnetism. He put a compass needle and a wire side by side. Then he passed an electric current through the wire. Imagine his surprise – and embarrassment – when the compass needle swung round!

What Oersted had found – by accident – was a really important discovery:

When a current flows through a wire, the wire has a magnetic field round it.

The compass needle was a small magnet. It was affected by the magnetic field round the wire. That's why it swung round.

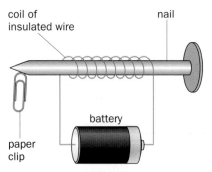

When a current flows through a single wire the magnetic field around it is very weak. If the wire is made into a coil the field is stronger. Putting a **core** of iron inside the coil makes the field even stronger! The core here is a nail.

You will remember that you can show the magnetic field around a bar magnet by sprinkling iron filings round it.

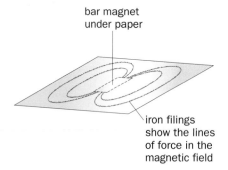

A coil of wire behaves like a bar magnet when a current flows though it. One end of the coil behaves like a magnet's north pole, and the other like a south pole. Changing the direction of the current changes the poles round.

If the core inside an electromagnet is steel, it tends to keep its magnetism even after the current has been switched off. If the core is made of soft iron, the magnetism disappears on switch-off.

1 What affected the compass needle in Oersted's experiment? ▲

2 A coil of wire behaves like a magnet when a current flows through it. What could you do to make the magnetic effect stronger? ▲

3 What would you need to make an electromagnet? Explain how you would control it once you have made it. ▲

4 Explain how you can demagnetise a piece of iron. What is happening to the poles at the end of the iron as you withdraw it from the coil?

DID YOU KNOW?

➲ You can magnetise a piece of iron by putting it in a coil of wire and passing a direct current through the wire.

➲ You can demagnetise a piece of iron by placing it inside a coil of wire carrying alternating current, and then slowly withdrawing it.

Electromagnets are used to do many different jobs.

Huge electromagnets are used in **scrapyard cranes**. They are powerful enough to lift cars. They are also useful for sorting out scap iron from other metals.

You can see the channels containing the electromagnets to lift the train clear of the track – look, no wheels!

Electric bell

The electric bell uses an electromagnet which is made to switch on and off automatically. The electromagnet attracts a piece of soft iron with a small hammer on the end of it. As long as the bell switch is pressed, the hammer keeps vibrating against the gong.

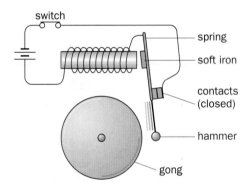

The contacts start off closed. When the switch is pushed, a current flows through the coils. The electromagnet attracts the iron, and the hammer hits the gong. But because of this movement, the contacts separate.

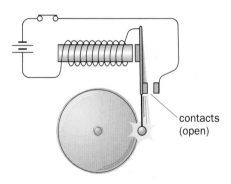

Now that the contacts are open, no current flows. The electromagnet no longer attracts the iron. The spring pulls the armature back into the starting position, and the contacts close. Then the current starts to flow again.

1 Why are electromagnets useful
   a in scrapyards
   b in hospitals? ▲
2 Imagine you were a crane driver in a scrapyard. Explain exactly what you would do to lift a car across the yard with an electromagnet.
3 In the electric bell,
   a What material would the coil be made from?
   b Why is soft iron used for the core of the coil?
   c Why does no current flow until the switch is pressed?
   d Why does current stop flowing as the hammer moves towards the gong?
4 **Try to find out** in what way an electric buzzer would be different from an electric bell.

DID YOU KNOW?

➲ A special kind of motor, which uses electricity and magnetism, drives Maglev forwards.

➲ Computers on Maglev control the height at which it rides. By altering the power of the electromagnets, they keep it 15 mm above the track.

If you had to build a big, strong electromagnet, what would you do? Which material would you use to make the core? How many turns of wire would you wind round it? What size of current would you use? All of these things matter.

Here are the results of some students' experiments. They will help you work out the answers to these questions. The electromagnets in the diagrams are all different. The number of paper clips which they can lift varies, too. You can tell how strong the magnet is from the number of paper clips it supports.

Two things to notice:

1   The electromagnet cores are all the same size.
2   When the current is switched off, the paper clips drop from the iron-cored magnet, but not from the steel-cored one.

Electromagnet	1	2	3	4	5	6
Core material	iron	iron	iron	iron	iron	steel
Number of turns in coil	10	20	20	30	20	20
Current	1A	0.5A	1A	1A	1.5A	1.5A
Number of paper clips lifted	2	3	4	6	10	7

Electromagnet	7	8	9	10	11	12
Core material	steel	iron	iron	iron	iron	iron
Number of turns in coil	30	20	20	20	20	20
Current	1A	2A	2.5A	3A	3.5A	4A
Number of paper clips lifted	5	17	22	26	28	28

1   Draw a circuit diagram for the experiment described on this page. ▲
2   Describe how the students would have carried out their experiment. ▲
3   How did the students judge how strong each magnet was? ▲
4   What three things affected the strength of the electromagnets?
5   If you wanted to find out how the number of turns affects the strength, which three magnets would you compare? Why did you choose them? How does the number of turns affect the strength?
6 a   Which magnets would allow you to find out how the strength of a magnet depends on the current?
  b   Draw and complete the graph on the right for iron-coiled magnets only with 20 turns of coil.
  c   'The bigger the current, the stronger the electromagnet.' Is this true?

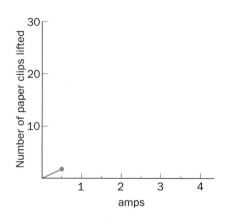

Redraw and complete this graph for all the electromagnets with **iron cores** and **20 turns** in the coil

When electronic engineers start to work on a design task, instead of thinking about the hundreds of components that they may use, they look at **electronic systems**.

They look at the behaviour of the system as a whole and the job it has to do.

All electronic systems have three parts: an **input**, a **processor**, and an **output**. The processor modifies information received from the input and may make decisions as a result. Some processors have an extra part, a **memory**, which can store information. Looking at what each **part** of the system does helps you to understand how a system works as a whole. Here are three examples of electronic systems.

system diagram

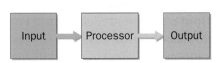

	INPUT	PROCESSOR	OUTPUT
CALCULATOR	keyboard	integrated circuit with memory	digital and numerical display
	converts key presses into electrical signals – each key is a separate switch	processes and stores information	displays the results
AUTOMATIC CAMERA	light meter	integrated circuit	shutter motor
	light alters resistance of a light dependent resistor (LDR)	calculates the exposure time from the LDR current	shutter opens for the required time
CD PLAYER	pick up	amplifier	loudspeakers
	converts information from the laser light reflected from the disc into electrical signals	makes small electrical signals larger	converts electrical energy into sound energy in the headset loudspeakers

1 What are the three parts that all electronic systems have? ▲

2 Explain how a CD player works by describing what each part of the electronic system does. ▲

3 Which part of the electronic system of a tape player would be different from that of a record player?

Electronic systems are often used to convert changes in their environment to something which is more controllable or measurable.

Input components detect these environmental changes, which then produce electrical signals in the rest of the system. Different input components detect different things:

Light

Light dependent resistor (LDR) The resistance of a LDR depends on how much light falls on it. In the dark, it has a high resistance, and so only a small amount of current can flow through it.

Solar cells Convert about 15% of the energy from light to electrical energy. This energy can be used to produce an electrical signal, but is also enough to power things like calculators.

Temperature

Thermistors are like LDRs but respond to heat. The resistance of a thermistor falls when it is heated. This allows a larger current to flow.

Thermocouples convert heat energy to a small amount of electrical energy.

Sound

One type of *microphone* contains a magnet and a coil of wire. Sound waves move the coil along the magnet and this generates a tiny electric current.

Movement

Switches only conduct electricity when they are closed. *Tilt switches* contain a blob of mercury near the switch contacts. When the switch is tilted, mercury flows across the contacts and completes the circuit.

Magnetic field

Reed switch The 'reed' is made of steel, so that the switch can be closed or opened by a magnetic force. This force can be from a permanent magnet or from an electromagnet. Reed switches can be either normally 'open' (the magnet closes the switch) or normally 'closed' (the magnet opens the switch).

Moisture

A moisture sensor consists of two contacts close together. When the contacts are dry, resistance is high. When water lies between the contacts the resistance falls and current flows.

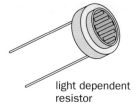
light dependent resistor

solar cell

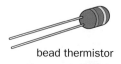
bead thermistor

microphone

reed switch

(normally open type)

QUESTIONS

1 What do all the components have in common for
   a what they detect
   b what they produce? ▲
2 What does an LDR detect? ▲
3 If a fire alarm was designed to detect smoke or fire, which two sensors might you use? ▲
4 A fridge-freezer is designed so that the motor will switch on when either the fridge or the freezer gets too warm. What sensors would be needed?
5 The heater in a washing machine only comes on after the door has been closed and the machine has filled with water. What two input components would be needed?

DiD YOU KNOW?

⊃ In a metal detector, a high frequency radio wave is transmitted from a coil into the soil. If metal is present in the soil, it is detected by altering the frequency of the processor circuit.

If metal is present the operator hears a change of pitch in the headphones.

Input components detect changes in the environment and send electrical signals to the processor. The processor then sends a signal to the output.

Output components receive these electrical signals and react. Different components react in different ways. In designing an electronic system, you need to choose the most useful component for the job.

Lamps and LEDs

In some calculators and digital clocks, electrical energy is converted into light in a *light emitting diode* (LED). This shines when a current passes through it. Compared with a normal lamp, it works on a smaller current and it produces less heat. LEDs are very useful for indicator lamps.

Loudspeakers, buzzers, and sirens

In *loudspeakers, buzzers,* and *alarm sirens*, electrical energy is converted into sound energy.

loudspeaker

Relays make a circuit with a small current control a circuit with a large current. When a current flows in the first circuit, the electromagnet attracts the switch contact bar and closes the gap in the second circuit. The second circuit may include a heater or motor.

Heaters

The large current in the relay second circuit may be used to operate a *heater*.

Motors

Electrical *motors* can convert electrical energy in the relay second circuit into movement. This could operate wheels or fans.

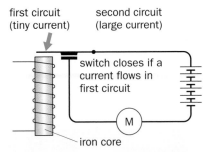

first circuit (tiny current)   second circuit (large current)

switch closes if a current flows in first circuit

M

iron core

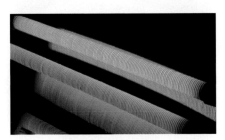

motor

QUESTIONS

1 What do all output devices
   a detect
   b produce? ▲
2 What kind of output device could you use
   a to warn you of a fire
   b to let you know that the freezer was switched on? ▲
3 Write a sentence on how each output component could be used around the school.
4 Which input and output components would you combine to
   a warn you that the fridge is not working
   b turn on an outdoor light when it gets dark
   c warn you that someone has broken into your house? ▲

DiD YOU KNOW?

➲ Linear activators are devices that convert electrical signals into motion in a straight line. The one shown here is used to make automatic fine adjustments to the rudder in a jet aircraft. It is controlled by the aircraft's flight computer. It drives a hydraulic valve that moves the aircraft rudder.

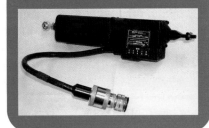

In the early days of electronics, circuits used capacitors, diodes, resistors, and transistors. Capacitors could store electric charge. Diodes only let current flow through a circuit in one direction. Resistors were used to resist, or reduce, the current flowing through other components. Transistors could be used in two ways, as an amplifier, or as an on-off switch.

Nowadays, thousands of these components can be produced on one tiny chip of silicon the size of a pinhead. These tiny packages of components with connections fitted to them are called integrated circuits (ICs).

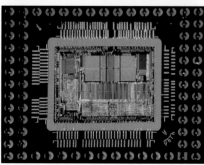

Integrated circuits can be made which do all sorts of jobs. They fall into two main types, **analogue** and **digital**. Analogue processors, such as amplifiers, use electrical signals to represent continuous physical quantities. Digital processors, such as counters and logic gates, consist of switching circuits which can be either 'on' or 'off'.

Amplifiers

The most important use of operational amplifiers (op amps) is to amplify (or multiply) DC and AC voltages. They are analogue processors. They carry information on the loudness and pitch of a sound as the amplitude and frequency of their electrical voltages. The **gain** (multiplication factor) of an amplifier can be 1000 or even 100 000!

By connecting it in a different way, an op amp can be used to add a number of voltages. This type of circuit can be used as a mixer, to combine microphone, electric guitar, and special effect outputs for audio use.

A **power driver** is an amplifier chip which can handle very high power throughput. It can incorporate various protection circuits to prevent system damage, for example from low voltage, high current, or high temperatures.

Older style circuit boards contain a mixture of separate components: resistors, capacitors, transistors, and others. They are still used alongside integrated circuits.

DID YOU KNOW?

➲ In 1904 Ambrose Fleming invented the first electronic component, a rectifier valve. This consisted of two metal electrodes in a glass bulb containing a vacuum. Large and expensive, it was eventually replaced by the much smaller and cheaper junction diode.

➲ The transistor was developed in 1947. It replaced the triode valve.

➲ Miniaturisation now enables large numbers of diodes and transistors to be incorporated into semiconductor chips.

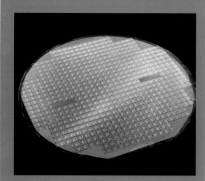

This disc of the semiconductor material, silicon, has around 300 microcircuits (or silicon chips) etched onto its surface. Each chip is sliced off, and fitted into a mounting with connectors to become an integrated circuit.

1 How are an analogue and a digital processor different in the way they process electrical information? ▲

2 Draw a system diagram to show what would be needed to convert signals from a DVD player into a form you could hear.

3 In a hi-fi amplifier what would be the difference in the input and output signals
   a in amplitude
   b in frequency?

4 What input, processor, and output components would you choose for a public address system? Draw a system diagram.

Logic

Some processors are able to make decisions. But they are not like human beings. Electronic systems can't think!

One way human beings come to a decision is to use reasoning, or **logic**. We say a decision is 'logical' if it seems sensible. What Tim says in the drawing opposite is not **logical**. The weather doesn't affect what day it is. Tony's conclusion is reasonable. He uses logic.

Digital processors use a more simple form of logic: **binary** logic. At any one time they decide between only two alternatives, the numbers '0' and '1'. But what do '0' and '1' mean? If you asked if current was flowing, the answer could be 'no' (0), or 'yes' (1). If you asked about the temperature it could be 'cold' (0) or 'hot' (1).

This table shows how different types of information could be coded in binary form.

binary code	simple choice	current	voltage	switch	LDR	therm-istor	moisture meter	buzzer	LED
0	no	low/zero	low/zero	off	dark	cold	dry	silent	unlit
1	yes	high	high	on	light	hot	wet	buzzes	lit

input count	output 3	output 2	output 1
0	0	0	0
1	0	0	1
2	0	1	0
3	0	1	1

Counters

Because a single processor can have an output of '0' or '1', you can use it to count. You can count to higher numbers if the output of the first processor is connected to the input of a second, and so on. A two-stage counter can count up to four (including the '0'). For a three-stage unit, you can count up to eight (including the '0'). A four-stage counter could count up to sixteen.

Numerical displays

A common type of number display is the seven segment type. You can see it in calculators, or petrol pumps or shop tills. Each segment can be on (black) or off (clear).

For the number 1, only segments A and B are 'on'.
For the number 2, G, A, E, D, and C would be 'on'.

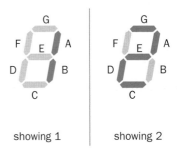

showing 1   showing 2

1 Look at the counter table above. If you used three LEDs as the output of a counter, make drawings to show which would be lit for the numbers 1, 4, and 6. ▲

2 For a four LED counter, make drawings to show which would be lit for numbers 5, 8, 11, and 14? ▲

3 How many could you count up to with ten LEDs?

4 Make a table with the numbers 0 to 9 down the left hand side, and the letters A to G across the top. For the seven segment numerical display, mark which segments, must be on to display each number.

4 **Try to find out** how Morse code uses a system of dots (0) and dashes (1) to transmit information.

Logic gates are the decision-makers of electronic processors. They are called 'gates' because they have to receive the correct input signals before they will let information through to the output. The name of a gate gives a clue to which input signals are required before a high (logic 1) signal is passed to the output. A **truth table** shows the possible outputs of a gate for all its possible inputs.

NOT gates

The simplest gate is called a **NOT gate**. It has one input and one output connection. Its output is 'high' (logic 1, or 'on') when its input is *not* high (logic 0, or 'off').

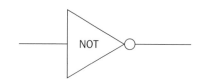

input	output
0	1
1	0

Some yachts have an automatic anchor light for when nobody is on board. It comes on when it gets dark, and turn off again when it gets light in the morning. When it gets dark, the LDR is at '0'. The NOT gate converts this to a '1' output. The lamp at the top of the mast then lights up.

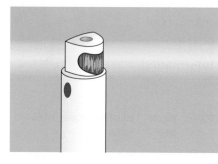

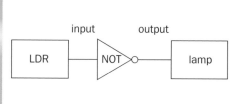

AND gates

An **AND gate** has two inputs and one output connection. The output is high (logic 1, or 'on') only when the first *and* second input are high (logic 1, or 'on').

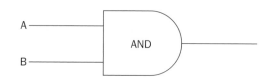

input A	input B	output
0	0	0
0	1	0
1	0	0
1	1	1

Giant presses like the one on the right exert very large forces. The operator has to press two switches at the same time to start the machine.

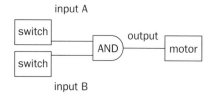

---

1 Draw the truth table for a NOT gate.

2 You want to make a light which will come on automatically when it gets dark. Draw a system diagram to show what type of input, gate, and output you would use. What will the input to, and output from the gate be when it is
 a day
 b night?

3 Draw the truth table for an AND gate.

4 How could you use an AND gate to modify the light in question **2** so that you could switch off the light permanently when you were away?

5 Draw a system diagram for an AND gate followed by a NOT gate. Draw a truth table for this combination of gates.

OR gates

An OR gate also has two inputs and one output. The output is high (logic 1, or 'on') when the first input is high (logic 1, or 'on'), *or* when the second input is high (logic 1, or 'on'), *or* when both are high.

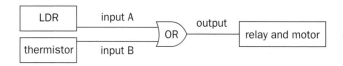

input A	input B	output
0	0	0
0	1	1
1	0	1
1	1	1

A gardener designs a system which draws the greenhouse blinds if it gets very bright ...

... or very hot.

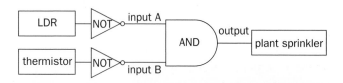

A gardener decides that it is best for a plant sprinkler to operate only when it is dark ...

... and cool.

This dishwasher has a LED system to indicate which part of the programme is operating.

The compressor of this fridge-freezer switches on when either the fridge or the freezer gets too warm.

Some quiz shows use a system of switches and gates to ensure that only one person can buzz at a time.

1 Draw the truth table for an OR gate.

2 In the case of the greenhouse blinds above, what would be the logic state of the output from the OR gate when the greenhouse was
  a bright and cool
  b dull and cool
  c bright and hot
  d dull and hot? Why is a relay necessary?

3 In the sprinkler system above, what would be the logic state of the output from the AND gate when it was
  a light and warm
  b light and cool
  c dark and cool? Would the sprinkler be on for **a**, **b**, or **c**?

4 In this sprinkler system, how could you redesign the layout to use one less NOT gate?

5 Design a smoke detector which will sound an alarm if the room gets hot, or if smoke causes the surroundings to get dark.

6 Draw a system diagram for a burglar alarm which will operate when a window is opened, or when a light is turned on. Label the input, processor, and output devices.

7 For the three photographs above, draw labelled system diagrams to show how the input devices, gates, and output devices are used.

8 Draw a system diagram for an OR gate followed by a NOT gate. Draw a truth table for this combination of gates.

The growth of the human population, and the increased use of natural resources, are having serious effects on the Earth. Pollution of air, water, and the land, along with the destruction of natural habitats, is reducing the number of animal and plant species. Many species have disappeared for ever – they are extinct.

Conservation is a way of keeping the number of animals and plant species at a steady level, but not everyone is prepared to give up a comfortable lifestyle to pay for it.

Living things interact with each other and with their environment. This affects where animals and plants live and how many live there. Those that can't adapt to change don't survive. Evolution is caused by changes called mutations in the genes of a population, usually as a result of natural selection. Sometimes evolution results in the production of a new species.

The Scottish wildcat is one animal that may soon disappear.

Environment is a scientific word for surroundings. You are probably reading this in your school environment or your home environment. Your environment provides you with air to breathe, water to drink, and a suitable temperature in which to live. These are the physical or **abiotic** (non living) parts of your environment.

Your life is also affected by other living things. These could be the people in your class, your family, your pets, and even bacteria in the air. These are called **biotic** (living) factors. Living things, together with the abiotic parts of their environment, form an **ecosystem**. In an ecosystem many different cycles happen. These help keep the environment the same as years goes by.

The picture shows some biotic and abiotic factors that can affect the environment.

A woodland ecosystem. Soil gives water and minerals for plants to grow. Animals depend on the plants for shelter and for food.

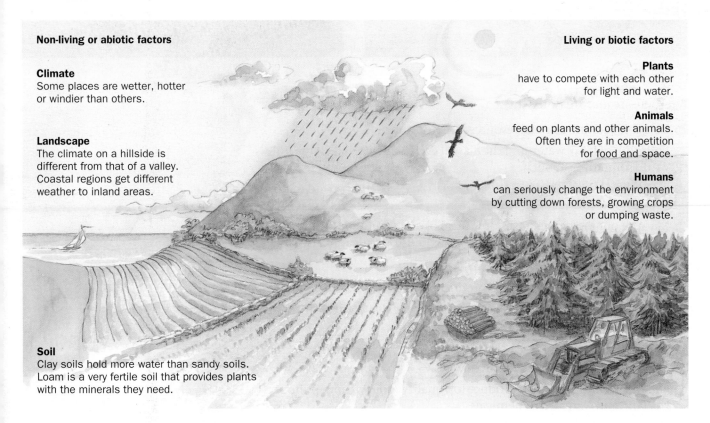

Non-living or abiotic factors

Climate
Some places are wetter, hotter or windier than others.

Landscape
The climate on a hillside is different from that of a valley. Coastal regions get different weather to inland areas.

Soil
Clay soils hold more water than sandy soils. Loam is a very fertile soil that provides plants with the minerals they need.

Living or biotic factors

Plants
have to compete with each other for light and water.

Animals
feed on plants and other animals. Often they are in competition for food and space.

Humans
can seriously change the environment by cutting down forests, growing crops or dumping waste.

1 What does 'environment' mean? ▲
2 Explain the difference between a biotic factor and an abiotic factor. ▲
3 a Describe the environment where you are reading this book.
   b Give two non living parts of this environment.
   c Give two living parts of this environment.
4 a What is an ecosystem?
   b Give an example of an ecosystem.
5 **Try to find out** the yearly temperature range for the area in which you live.

DID YOU KNOW?
➲ The study of ecosystems is called ecology. Scientists who study ecosystems are called ecologists.

Many of the things that humans do destroy the environment and the animals and plants which are part of it. The number of different animal and plant species is falling. Every year more species become extinct – gone forever.

Why must we protect the environment?

Most humans would rather see this ...

...than this.

But there are more reasons why.

- Valuable fuel and mineral resources are running out.
- Pollution of land, water, and the air will eventually poison all life unless we do something about it.
- Cutting down trees reduces the supply of oxygen to the air and removes shelter for wildlife.
- Many of our medicines have come from plants. There could be undiscovered plants which may provide the cure for deadly diseases.

How can we protect the environment?

- Buy 'environmentally friendly' products, especially cleaning materials.
- Look for biodegradable packaging that rots quickly when it is thrown away.
- Recycle as much of our waste as we can.
- Plant more trees as others are cut down.
- Organic farming methods produce top quality food without polluting the land and water with chemicals.
- Planned land use – where possible, houses and roads should be built with the interests of wildlife and humans in mind.
- Creating and maintaining national parks and nature reserves to keep habitats protected.

DID YOU KNOW?

- Large predators such as the brown bear, the wolf, and the Northern lynx once lived in Scotland. They are now extinct, all because of humans.

1 a What does extinct mean?
  b Give one example of an animal that is extinct in Scotland. ▲
2 Tropical rainforests are home to many undiscovered plants and animals. Explain why we should be concerned about cutting down trees in tropical rainforests. ▲
3 What can you do to try and protect the environment?
4 If you were able to pass one law about protecting wildlife what would it be?
5 **Try to find out** what things can be recycled.

Humans first appeared on Earth about 2 million years ago. For much of this time we have shared our planet with millions of other plant and animal species. We form part of ecosystems, just as other organisms do. However as our numbers have grown we are having a greater and greater impact on ecosystems.

Two thousand years ago most of Britain was covered with trees. Forests were cleared to provide space for growing crops and grazing animals.

Industry needs fuels and other materials from the ground. Mining and quarrying damage the landscape. Dinorwig quarry stopped operation in 1969.

The Andes rise above the industrial smog in Santiago, Chile. On days like this you cannot see the Andes from within the city.

Waste chemicals are sometimes dumped into rivers or the sea. About 30 million tonnes of household rubbish are buried in the ground each year.

To feed the growing human population, farmers use fertilizers to help crops grow. But fertilizers can get into rivers where they encourage the growth of algae. This algae uses up all the oxygen in the water so fish die.

Farmers use pesticides to kill insects and other pests. Unfortunately pesticides can get into food chains and kill other things as well.

1 Why are humans having a greater impact on ecosystems?
2 Why were forests cleared?
3 Make a list of the things that spoil your school environment.
4 Explain why fertilizers can be good and bad for the environment.
5 **Try to find out** where your household rubbish ends up.

DiD YOU KNOW?
➲ Pet cemeteries have to be licensed as landfill sites.

Twenty-seven thousand years ago the climate in Scotland was much colder than it is today. Huge animals such as the woolly rhinoceros and the hairy mammoth roamed the country in large numbers. Both of these animals are now totally extinct: there are none alive anywhere in the world. We only know they existed because fossils have been found. In the case of the hairy mammoth, whole animals have been discovered frozen in the ice in Siberia. Evidence from fossils gives us a good idea of what the woolly rhinoceros looked like. Whole bodies of hairy mammoths have been found in the Siberian deep freeze.

Extinct? – not quite!

Reindeer became extinct in Scotland in the 12th century. In 1952 they were reintroduced and now number about 100 animals.

Wolves were common in Scotland until the mid-18th century. They became extinct because their woodland habitats were destroyed and farmers killed them to protect their farm animals. There has been talk of reintroducing the wolf to Scotland but nothing has happened yet - although some people claim that wolves have already been reintroduced secretly!

The corncrake – a success story in Scotland

The corncrake is a ground nesting bird which makes a very distinctive sound – a bit like a fingernail dragging over the teeth of a comb. Since the start of the twentieth century the corncrake has steadily declined in numbers. This is mainly because farm machinery and more frequent grass cutting for hay and silage have reduced the habitats corncrakes need.

Today the corncrake is very rare and it only exists in the Western Isles of Scotland. However recent research by the RSPB has found a way of making farmland better for corncrakes. With the help of crofters, corncrake numbers are increasing for the first time in a hundred years.

1 How do we know the woolly rhinoceros existed in Scotland? ▲
2 Explain why living things become extinct. ▲
3 Explain how wolves become extinct in Scotland. ▲
4 a Why did the numbers of corncrakes decline in the twentieth century?
  b Who has helped to prevent the corncrake becoming extinct in Scotland? ▲
5 **Try to find out** the names of some other animals that are now extinct in Scotland.

DID YOU KNOW?

There are three ways a species can become extinct:

➲ the environment changes too quickly

➲ a predator or disease kills them

➲ they can't compete for food.

Animals and plants have developed special features to help them cope with their way of life. They have become **adapted** to their environment.

Lions have strong teeth for tearing flesh and crushing bones.

Butterflies have long tubular mouths for sucking nectar.

Most flowers have colour and scent to attract insects for pollination.

Some living things have extra special adaptations to help them survive in a very harsh environment.

The polar bear

The polar bear lives in **arctic conditions** where it is very cold, especially in winter. It has lots of special features to help it live in a very cold climate.

Thick fur keeps the bear warm. The fur is **greasy** to keep it dry when it is swimming in icy water.

Under the skin is a thick layer of fat called **blubber**. This insulates the animal and provides a food store.

Small ears reduce heat loss.

White fur matches the surroundings. Young bears need camouflage for protection against predators.

Strong legs enable polar bears to swim and run fast after their prey.

Big feet spread the bear's weight on the snow and ice to stop it sinking.

1 Describe how
   a butterflies are adapted to collect nectar
   b flowers are adapted to pollinate. ▲
2 What are arctic conditions? ▲
3 How do these things help a polar bear?
   a small ears
   b a thick layer of blubber
   c big feet ▲
4 a Describe a polar bear's fur.
   b How does this help a polar bear survive?
5 **Try to find out** how other animals survive in arctic conditions

DiD YOU KNOW?
➲ Fish that live in the Arctic produce an antifreeze for their blood to help them survive in the ice-cold water.

109

Deserts are very harsh environments. Daytime temperatures can be over 70 °C, but at night temperatures can fall to below freezing. There is also very little water about. Despite these extreme conditions, some living things are adapted for life in these regions. Camels and cacti are good examples.

The camel

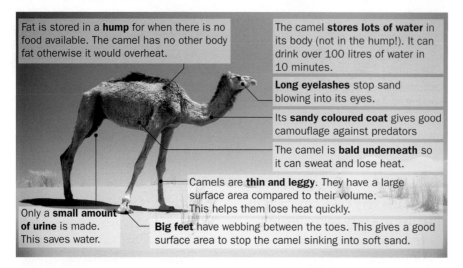

Fat is stored in a **hump** for when there is no food available. The camel has no other body fat otherwise it would overheat.

The camel **stores lots of water** in its body (not in the hump!). It can drink over 100 litres of water in 10 minutes.

Long eyelashes stop sand blowing into its eyes.

Its **sandy coloured coat** gives good camouflage against predators

The camel is **bald underneath** so it can sweat and lose heat.

Camels are **thin and leggy**. They have a large surface area compared to their volume. This helps them lose heat quickly.

Only a **small amount of urine** is made. This saves water.

Big feet have webbing between the toes. This gives a good surface area to stop the camel sinking into soft sand.

The cactus

Their leaves are reduced to **spines**. This cuts down the surface area so less water is lost.

Water is stored in the fleshy, green stem. The stem is covered in a **thick waxy cuticle** to stop water loss.

The cactus has a **spreading root system** that stetches out a long way from the plant. The roots can then take in dew that forms on the ground.

1 Describe a desert environment. ▲
2 Why do camels have
  a big feet
  b long eyelashes
  c a bald tummy
  d a hump? ▲

3 Explain how a camel can go for long periods without drinking water. ▲
4 Describe the adaptations that help the cactus survive in desert conditions. ▲
5 **Try to find out** how heather is adapted to living on moorland.

A habitat such as a moorland usually looks the same year after year. This is because it is managed by humans to stay that way. If an area of land is left alone for a hundred years, competition between plants for light, water, and minerals in the soil will eventually result in it becoming covered with trees.

This is what happens to an area of bare soil in northern Britain over a long period of time. At each stage, the plants are adapted to make the most of their chances of survival.

1 The first plants (called **colonizers**) are weeds such as chickweed. These plants have a short life cycle – their seeds are produced quickly before the parent plant dies.

2 These are soon replaced by grasses. Their spreading roots and stems quickly cover the soil.

3 Soon, tall weeds including foxgloves and ferns replace the grasses by cutting out their light.

4 Seeds of shrubs such as heather and gorse have now germinated and won the competition for light by forming a dense blanket under which few other plants can grow.

5 Small trees begin to grow. Seeds from trees like the Scots Pine and Silver Birch will have been carried by the wind to land in the open areas between the shrubs.

6 As the years go by, the trees grow to form a high canopy (here at Crianlarich). Leaves of the pine tree are shaped like needles and have a thick waxy coat. These adaptations help to reduce water loss.

1 Why do moorlands look the same year after year? ▲
2 What are colonizers? How do they adapt to a changing environment? ▲
3 Explain how heather wins the competition against grasses and other low lying plants. ▲
4 Explain why Scotland is no longer covered in pine forests.
5 **Try to find out** what 'ecological succession' means.

DID YOU KNOW?
➲ Grazing by domestic and wild animals keeps the landscape as it is. Without human activity, Scotland would eventually be covered in forests of birch and pine trees.

Evolution is one way of explaining why there are so many different living things on Earth. When something **evolves** it changes and improves on something that went before.

Evolution of vertebrates

The first living things appeared on Earth more than 500 million years ago. They were very simple but they could reproduce. Some of the young were different to their parents. These differences meant they could survive better and breed, passing on their differences to their offspring. Over billions of years more changes and improvements have led to all the different animals and plants alive today.

This diagram shows how vertebrates could have evolved. Notice how mammals and birds both evolved from reptiles.

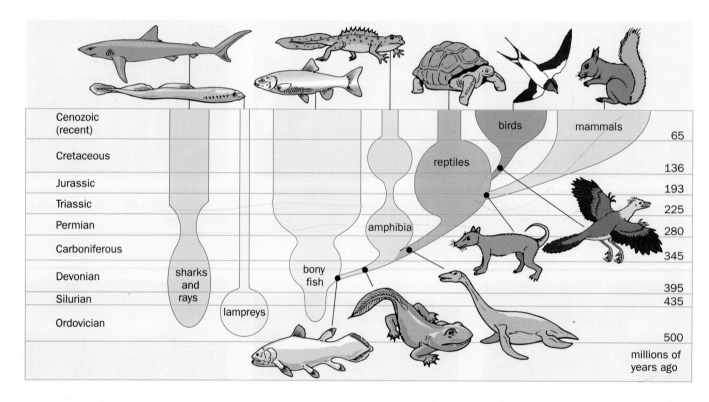

Cenozoic (recent)	birds mammals	65
Cretaceous	reptiles	136
Jurassic		193
Triassic		225
Permian	amphibia	280
Carboniferous		345
Devonian	bony fish	395
Silurian		435
Ordovician		500
	sharks and rays lampreys	millions of years ago

Birds are believed to have evolved from a group of flesh-eating dinosaurs. At some stage in their history scales evolved into feathers, probably to help with temperature control. The evolution of feathers meant they were able to fly. This photograph shows a fossil of the first known bird, *Archaeopteryx*. It was about the size of a magpie and lived about 150 million years ago. *Archaeopteryx* could fly but not as well as birds today.

1 What does 'evolution' mean? ▲
2 When did the first life forms live on Earth? ▲
3 What did birds evolve from? ▲
4 Humans are mammals. What have we evolved from? ▲

5 What do you think led to the evolution of birds from dinosaur ancestors? ▲
6 **Try to find out** where the first fossils of *Archeopteryx* were found.

DID YOU KNOW?

➔ Pterodactyls, flying reptiles, are totally unrelated to birds. They were able to fly using large flaps of skin connecting their hind and fore limbs – not feathers.

The theory of evolution suggests that all living things on Earth gradually evolved over millions of years rather than just appearing suddenly. A scientists called Charles Darwin suggested how evolution might happen. He called it his theory of **natural selection**. Natural selection means that those animals and plants that are best suited to their surroundings will survive and pass on their advantage to their young.

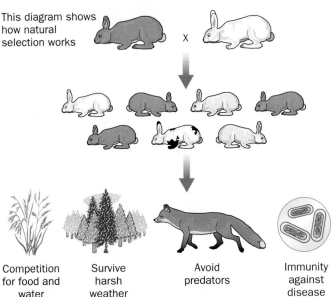

This diagram shows how natural selection works

Animals and plants have lots of offspring

Not all offspring are the same - there is variation

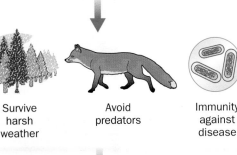

Competition for food and water

Survive harsh weather

Avoid predators

Immunity against disease

Some offspring are better suited to changes in the environment

Only the best adapted survive. This is called 'survival of the fittest'. The population stays roughly the same.

Charles Darwin (1809–1882) published his theory of evolution by natural selection in 1859.

Evidence for evolution

Most of the evidence for evolution comes from fossils. Fossils are any sort of preserved remains of an animal or plant. They tell us what animals and plants looked like and how long ago they lived. Generally the deeper in the ground a fossil is found, the older it is. The Grand Canyon in Arizona is the deepest crack in the Earth's surface. It is about a mile deep with young rocks at the top and the oldest rocks at the bottom. The canyon has lots of fossils. They are found in the order in which the animals and plants lived on Earth. This is called a **fossil record**. Near the top, dinosaurs fossils have been found. Halfway down the fossils of fish appear. At the bottom there are no fossils at all. Gaps in the fossil record are called **missing links**.

1 Who was Charles Darwin? ▲
2 a What is natural selection?
  b Explain how natural selection works. ▲
3 What is a fossil? ▲
4 Explain what is meant by a fossil record. ▲
5 **Try to find out** what a 'missing link' is.

DID YOU KNOW?

○ The most probable reason for the extinction of the dinosaurs is this.

The dinosaurs were unable to adapt when the temperature of the world dropped quite suddenly. The huge herbivores such as Brachiosaurus simply died of cold, and the carnivores like Tyrannosaurus that fed on them starved to death.

A **mutation** is a change in a chromosome or a gene which alters the way an organism develops. Strange, new characteristics appear which make the individual different from the rest of the population. Mutations usually happen when cells are dividing and DNA is copying itself.

Chromosome mutations

When gametes are made in the sex organs there is a chance that changes in the number or structure of chromosomes can happen. Some chromosomes break and genes are lost.

Sometimes pairs of chromosomes don't separate properly when sex cells are made. Both chromosomes go into the same sex cell. This kind of chromosome mutation causes **Down's syndrome**. A woman produces an egg containing 24 chromosomes instead of 23. When the egg is fertilized, the baby has 47 chromosomes instead of 46. Having an extra chromosome causes physical and mental problems for the sufferer.

Gene mutations

A gene mutation is a chemical change which alters the structure of DNA and so changes the message carried by a gene.

Cystic fibrosis is a disease caused by a gene mutation. The gene that controls the production of mucus in the lungs is altered. Instead of being runny, the mucus is thick and can't be easily cleared from the airways. Bacteria get stuck causing chest infections.

Mutations and evolution

Most mutations are harmful, but some are useful: they cause **evolution**.

Occasionally a mutation gives an individual an advantage over the others in the population.

For example, bacteria mutate to produce individuals that are resistant to antibiotics. The mutant lives and the 'normal' bacteria die. A new, 'resistant strain' of bacteria is the result. This causes big problems in hospitals.

Someone with Down's syndrome has an extra chromosome at pair 21.

Physiotherapy helps to clear the lungs of a person with cystic fibrosis.

Mutations have made some wild rats resistant to rat poison. These rats survive and pass on their mutant genes. So now, more and more rats are resistant to poison.

1 a What is a mutation?
  b When do mutations happen? ▲
2 a How many chromosomes does a person with Down's syndrome have in each of their cells?
  b Explain how this happens. ▲

3 Why are people with cystic fibrosis likely to have chest infections? ▲
4 Explain how mutations can lead to evolution.
5 Try to find out the name of some other diseases caused by mutations. (These are called genetic diseases.)

DiD YOU KNOW?

Mutations happen naturally. However the chances of a mutation are increased if you expose yourself to...

⊃ **X-rays** or **ultra-violet** light
⊃ chemicals like those found in **cigarette smoke** which cause cancer
⊃ nuclear radiation.

Going even further

Within this second book you will have studied something of electronics and refreshed your knowledge of sound. Sound is a basic element of science and has always been with us - right from the big-bang. Music is a 'pleasant' development of this! Electronics as a science has been with us for less than a hundred years. Sound becomes music and electronics provides us with the ability to record this music for future listening and appreciation. You will all have your favourite tapes or CDs and no doubt you will share them with your friends.

The National Centre of Excellence in Traditional Music is based at Plockton High School in Ross-shire. Here, secondary school students from all over Scotland learn about Scottish traditional music as part of their studies. They use traditional instruments such as the pipes and harp. In helping to maintain the musical tradition and to share it they have to make best use of modern-day technology. During their course the students make music CDs in the Centre's recording studio.

The Centre is using modern-day technology to help with its aims of furthering the appreciation of traditional Scottish music - it's a very practical example of the application of science. One of the further pages introduces the *trebuchet* - which **was** modern in its day! And that's what this chapter is all about: exploring more how science affects us in our everyday lives; past, present, and future.

Scientific evidence shows that life on Earth appeared relatively quickly. Scientists therefore believe that life could occur on any planet similar to Earth that orbits a Sun-like star. Recent evidence that life may once have existed on Mars supports this idea.

Scientists have been looking for evidence of intelligent life out in space for over half a century. They call these life forms 'extra terrestrial' or 'ET' for short. The search for ETs is called the **SETI** project – the Search for Extra-terrestrial Intelligence.

Huge radio telescopes like the one at Arecibo are used to search the areas around distant stars for any sign of 'non-natural' radio waves. The big difference between natural signals and those produced by a transmitter is their bandwidth (how wide they are). Narrow band signals are more likely to be artificially produced. It is these signals that SETI scientists are looking for.

If signals are ever found, communicating with the sender will be very difficult. Radio waves take about 4 years to reach us from *Alpha Centauri*, our nearest star, and 2 000 000 years from *Andromeda*, our nearest galaxy. Sending signals back takes just as long!

Why don't we just send a spacecraft?

The stars are simply too far away. Our best rockets travel at about 10 miles per second. Even to reach *Alpha Centauri* would take 60 000 years.

1 What is the SETI project and how long has it been going? ▲
2 Explain what would make a scientist think a signal was from an ET and not a natural source. ▲
3 Why, in the immediate future, is it unlikely that astronauts will be able to visit other planets looking for ETs? ▲
4 Explain why the 'little green men theory' was abandoned. ▲

DID YOU KNOW?

➲ In the 1960s, a scientist, Jocelyn Bell, noticed some strange radio signals coming from outer space. The signals were so regular and fast that no one thought they could be natural. The signal must be coming from extra terrestrials – 'little green men' as they became known.

The theory was soon abandoned. What Jocelyn Bell had discovered was a new type of star called a pulsar. These stars are called pulsars because they send out signals in regular pulses.

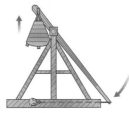

The trebuchet is prepared for firing by lifting the weighted end high into the air. The arm is held in place by a trigger mechanism.

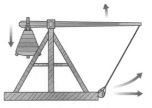

The sling is loaded with a missile. When the trigger is released, gravity causes the weighted end of the arm to fall. This causes the other end of the arm to move upwards. The sling begins to swing up and away from the trebuchet.

The trebuchet was once a terrible weapon of war. The Chinese invented it, and countries in the western world began using it in the 12th century. A trebuchet is a kind of unbalanced see-saw with a sling attached to hurl huge boulders and other missiles at the enemy.

A trebuchet is similar to a lever, with a heavy weight providing the force on one side of the pivot and the sling holding the missile supplying the force on the other side.

Trebuchets that throw humans (both dead and alive!) have been built. Diseased corpses were often slung over castle walls to spread disease amongst the besieged population. This was an early form of biological warfare. Soldiers, complete with armour and weapons, were often thrown over walls – whether or not they were in a fit state for fighting is not known!

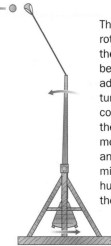

The sling rotates around the end of the beam. This additional turning force combines with the force of the moving arm and causes the missile to be hurled out of the sling.

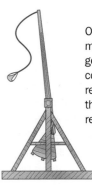

Once the missile has gone the arm comes to a rest ready for the sling to be reloaded.

DID YOU KNOW?

➲ Two Englishmen from Shropshire have built a 30 tonne trebuchet. It can throw a grand piano 115 metres, an upright piano 140 metres, and a dead pig 160 metres!

QUESTIONS

1 What is meant by 'unbalanced see-saw'? ▲
2 What force causes the weighted end of the trebuchet arm to fall when the trigger is released? ▲
3 Explain why it is an advantage to have the distance between the missile and the pivot greater than the distance between the weight and the pivot.

4 If a weight of 40 000 N was hung 2 m from the pivot at one end of a trebuchet arm, what force would be applied to the sling hanging 10 m from the other end?
5 Suggest how changing the length of the sling might affect the performance of the trebuchet.

Enzymes from microorganisms

Enzyme technology is a new industry. Large quantities of enzymes are collected from microorganisms such as bacteria and fungi. These enzymes are called **microbial enzymes**. Microbial enzymes have lots of uses in the food industry.

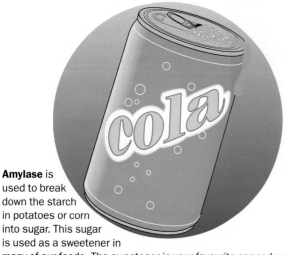

Amylase is used to break down the starch in potatoes or corn into sugar. This sugar is used as a sweetener in many of our foods. The sweetener in your favourite canned or bottled drink has probably been made by microbial enzymes.

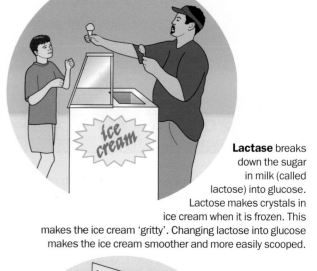

Lactase breaks down the sugar in milk (called lactose) into glucose. Lactose makes crystals in ice cream when it is frozen. This makes the ice cream 'gritty'. Changing lactose into glucose makes the ice cream smoother and more easily scooped.

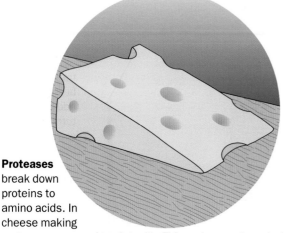

Proteases break down proteins to amino acids. In cheese making proteases are used to clot milk. This makes curds and whey. Cheese is made from the curds and the whey is thrown away.

Freshly squeezed fruit juice is cloudy because it contains a carbohydrate called pectin. **Pectinase** breaks down pectin into soluble sugars. Pectinases are added to crushed fruit such as apples and grapes to get more, clear juice out.

QUESTIONS

1 What are microbial enzymes? ▲
2 Explain how lactase makes ice cream easier to scoop. ▲
3 Milk clots when it is left to go sour. It separates into curds and whey. Why then do you think the cheese making industry uses enzymes to make curds and whey?

4 Explain the difference between natural and clear fruit juice.
5 See if you can find the names of
   a some foods that contain sweeteners
   b some soft scoop ice creams
   c some clear natural fruit juices.

DiD YOU KNOW?

➔ Enzymes in yeast turn sugar into alcohol during fermentation.

Smoke alarms go off when they detect smoke. A smoke alarm has two key components: a sensor which detects that there's smoke in a room, and a loud, shrill alarm designed to wake you up no matter how soundly you are sleeping. One kind of smoke detector contains a small amount of radioactive americium contained in an ionization chamber. Americium gives out particles because of its radioactivity.

An ionization chamber is made of two charged metal plates, one positive and the other negative. Between the two plates, oxygen and nitrogen molecules in the air are ionized when electrons are knocked out of the molecules by the radioactive particles. The result is that oxygen and nitrogen atoms become positive ions because each one is short of one electron. The positive ions flow toward the negative plate, and the negative ions flow towards the positive plate. This flow of charged ions is an electric current which flows all the time the alarm is switched on.

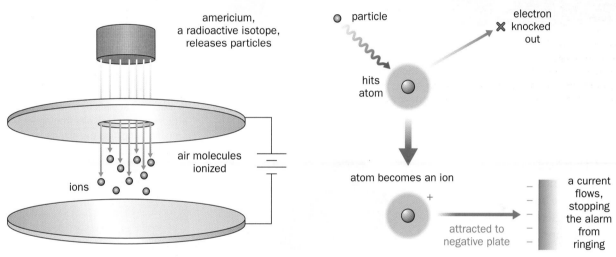

If smoke gets into the ionization chamber, smoke particles attach themselves to the charged ions and restore them to a neutral electrical state. This reduces the flow of electricity between the two plates in the ionization chamber, and when the electric current drops below a certain level, the alarm is switched on.

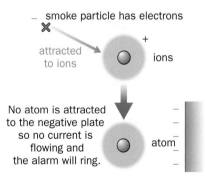

1 Explain how an electric current is set up in the ionization chamber of a smoke alarm. ▲

2 Explain how smoke causes a smoke alarm to go off. ▲

3 Americium is a radioactive element. Do you think using americium in smoke alarms is a sensible thing to do? Explain your answer.

DiD YOU KNOW?

➲ The radioactive element used in smoke detectors is americium-241, which was discovered by scientists during World War II. A smoke detector contains about 1/5000th of a gram of americium-241. Most of the radiation emitted by americium-241 is in the form of alpha particles which can't penetrate human skin.

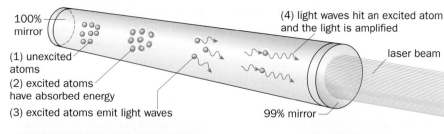

The word LASER stands for Light Amplification by Stimulated Emission of Radiation. A laser produces a very intense beam of light.

(1) unexcited atoms
(2) excited atoms have absorbed energy
(3) excited atoms emit light waves
100% mirror
99% mirror
(4) light waves hit an excited atom and the light is amplified
laser beam

Since light travels in straight lines, laser beams are dead straight. This, together with their intensity, makes them ideal for situations when pinpoint accuracy is required.

Lasers are used by surgeons to 'weld' body tissue together – for example in tricky eye operations.

On older vinyl records, sound vibrations are copied onto 'wobbles' on the sides of grooves which run around the record. The groove is an analogue of the sound: the bigger the wobble the louder the sound. The wobbles in the grooves are converted to electrical signals by a needle or stylus attached to a small electromagnet. An amplifier amplifies the signals and sends them to a loudspeaker.

CDs are different to vinyl: they are digital recordings. Instead of wobbly grooves, CDs have a pattern of microscopic bumps cut into them. The length of the bumps and the space between them determines the sound. The bumps are arranged in a long track of data, spiralling from the inside to the outside of the disc. The data track is incredibly small – only 0.5 microns wide (a micron is 1 000 000th of a metre). This is why CDs can hold so much data.

Inside a CD player there is a lot of computer technology. Safety warning – don't open a CD player to look inside.

A CD player finds and reads the data stored on a CD. As the disc spins, the pattern of bumps is read by a weak laser beam. The laser beam is focussed on the track of bumps and moves across the disc following the spiral track. The bumps reflect light differently, producing a reflected beam which is 'off' or 'on'. The reflected beam shines onto a light detector and decoder which converts it into an electric current, which can be amplified and passed to a loudspeaker.

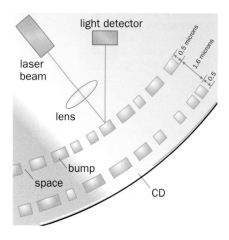

light detector, laser beam, lens, bump, space, CD, 0.5 microns, 1.6 microns, 0.5

DiD YOU KNOW?

⮕ DVDs work in a similar way to CDs but they can hold a lot more data. A standard DVD can hold about seven times more data than a CD does. This huge capacity means that a DVD has enough room to store a whole feature film, complete with 'surround sound' sound track.

1 Why are lasers suitable for accurate and delicate work? ▲
2 Explain why CDs can hold so much data. ▲
3 Describe how electrical signals are produced in
   a a vinyl record player
   b a CD player. ▲
4 What is the difference between a CD and a DVD? ▲

GM is short for **genetic modification**. Genetic modification is what biotechnologists do when they genetically engineer a living organism to behave differently. For example, with genetic modification bacteria are used to make human insulin.

"There's nothing new about GM. We've been selectively breeding animals and plants for centuries."

"I'm not sure, there's something a bit worrying about meddling with DNA. What about all that genetically modified pollen floating around. How do we know where it will land or what it will do if plants cross pollinate with it. It's unnatural!"

"It's really cool what scientists can do today. Soon there'll be loads of crops that can grow in the developing world without as much water or fertilizer, so people will no longer starve."

"These GM protesters have really got a point you know. The impact on our health and on the environment could be devastating. GM trials should stop now – it's better to be safe than sorry later."

"Oh come off it, these opponents to GM are nothing but a bunch of vandals who have cost taxpayers and farmers thousands of pounds because of crops they have ruined.

"But I saw a programme on TV that said the main problem was distributing food around the world, not producing enough of it. And if these scientists get it wrong we can't get the genes back as they were."

Scientists aren't out to poison us, they know what they are doing. Think how much the quality of our lives has been improved by scientific discoveries. There is just no evidence that GM foods are dangerous.

1 Make a list of the arguments for and against GM. ▲
2 What do you think about GM?

Like other industries, the chemical industry needs to make its products as cheaply and as quickly as possible. One way of speeding up a chemical reaction is to use a catalyst.

In the early 19th century a German chemist called **Fritz Haber** solved the problem of how to make ammonia on a large, commercial scale. Ammonia is used to make fertilizers such as ammonium nitrate. These fertilizers dissolve very fast and the nitrogen they contain can pass into plants quickly.

Nitrogen gas is taken out of the air by fractional distillation. Hydrogen is produced from water and natural gas. On their own nitrogen and hydrogen will mix but they won't react. However if an iron catalyst is used the two gases react to form ammonia.

The reaction is called the **Haber process**. This word equation summarizes the Haber process:

nitrogen + hydrogen → ammonia + heat

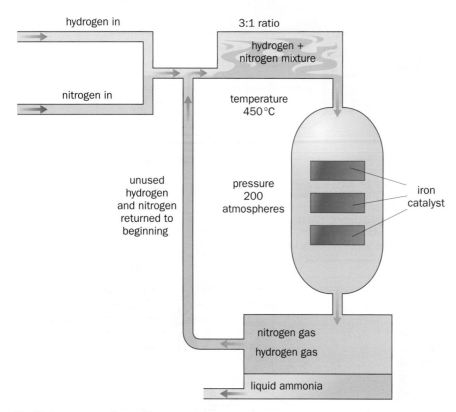

The Haber process for making ammonia

QUESTIONS

1 What catalyst is used in the Haber process? ▲
2 Describe the Haber process. ▲
3 Explain how the Haber process has lead to increased food production.

4 The Haber process is a chemical reaction. Explain how
   a raising the temperature
   b increasing the pressure speeds up a chemical reaction.

DiD YOU KNOW?
➲ The chemical reaction in the Haber process can happen at room temperature but very, very slowly. To make it happen faster, the temperature must be raised to around 450 °C. Also, more ammonia is produced if the pressure is increased to 200 atmospheres.

An automatic washing machine is very complicated. Logic gates are ideally suited for use in complicated pieces of machinery where there are several things to be monitored and controlled.

If a washing machine is to work properly

➲ its water supply must be controlled
➲ the water has to be at the right temperature
➲ it mustn't fill with water if the door is open.

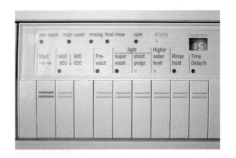

A suitable control system for a washing machine must have input sensors, logic gates (processors), and output components.

The diagram shows the logic circuit for an automatic washing machine.

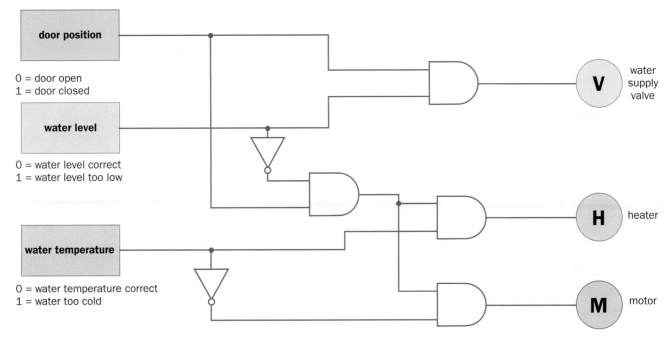

1 When the door is closed (output 1) AND the water level is low (output 1) the valve opens, letting the machine fill with water. When the water level is correct the sensor gives an output of 0 so the water valve closes.

2 When the door is closed (output 1) AND the water level is correct (output 0) AND the temperature is low (output 1) the water heater comes on. When the water temperature is high enough, the temperature sensor gives an output of 0 so the heater turns off.

3 Finally, when the door is closed (output 1) AND the water level is correct (output 0) AND the water temperature is correct (output 0) the motor turns the drum of the washing machine.

DiD YOU KNOW?
➲ Electronic switches can only handle tiny electric currents. So they can't directly switch on powerful things like motors and heaters. To get round this problem a **relay** is used. The electronic switch turns on the relay and this switches on the more powerful circuits.

QUESTIONS

1 Name
  a the input sensors
  b the logic gates
  c the output components in the logic circuit shown above. ▲

2 The water level sensor gives a '0' when the level is correct.
  a What gate is used to turn this into a '1'?
  b Why is this gate needed? ▲

3 **Try to find out** more about relays.

Most animals and plants that live in the sea can't survive out of water. The sea and the land are very different environments. Nature has had to make some clever changes to animals and plants, through evolution, to enable them to live on land all the time.

In water seaweed floats near the surface to get light. On land seaweed is floppy. This is because there is no **support** from the water. On land, even the smallest bodies need support. We have a skeleton inside our bodies. Insects have skeletons on the outside.

All living things contain large amounts of water – as much as 90%. To avoid **drying out** on land, animals and plants need a tough, waterproof skin.

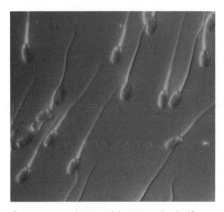

Sperms need something to swim in if they are going to successfully **fertilize** an egg. In the sea this is easy as there is plenty of water. On land however this is more of a problem. Animals and plants have come up with some clever solutions – the penis is probably the best!

Air warms up and cools down quicker than water. During the day there is a greater **temperature** range on land than in the sea. Animals especially need to be able to regulate their body temperature to keep cool in hot weather and warm when it is cold.

The sea provides everything that animals and plants need – dissolved gases, nutrients, and light for photosynthesis. On land these things are available but in separate places. Animals can move to get the things they need. Plants, however, have to get **water and nutrients** from the soil and light and gases from the air. To solve this problem, plants have evolved roots and shoots connected together by a transport system.

QUESTIONS

1 Make a list of the problems facing animals and plants that live on land. ▲
2 Why is sexual reproduction only possible in wet conditions? ▲
3 Explain why land plants have a transport system. ▲

4 The Blue Whale is the largest living thing in the sea. The African elephant is the largest land animal. Explain why a blue whale weighs as much as twenty five elephants. ▲
5 List some of the ways that you can cool down in hot weather and keep warm when it is cold.

DID YOU KNOW?
↪ Most mammals have legs under their bodies so they can move more easily on land. Amphibians live both on land and in water. Their legs are splayed out to the sides of their bodies.

Index

Index

Index